The Cowardly Lioness

JEAN · ROOK

The Cowardly Lioness

SIDGWICK & JACKSON
LONDON

First published in Great Britain in 1989 by
Sidgwick & Jackson Limited
1 Tavistock Chambers, Bloomsbury Way
London WC1A 2SG

ISBN 0-283-99830-X

Photoset by Rowland Phototypesetting Limited
Bury St Edmunds, Suffolk
Printed in Great Britain by
Mackays of Chatham PLC, Chatham, Kent

To my mother
I owe you my life. I owe you the
courage and strength to get on with
my life, and write this book.

Acknowledgements

To *Daily Express* Editor, Nicholas Lloyd, for turning a blind eye to the book-writing days I should have been in Fleet Street, and wasn't.

To my constant supporter, advisor, and unfailing sounding board, Alan Frame.

To my best friend and former secretary, Nicola Janson, who held my hand through cancer and the labour on the book, and to her then unborn baby, Victoria, who sat patiently through it all.

And to my new friend and secretary, Jill Shiel, for so nobly taking over where Victoria forced Nicky to leave off.

Contents

CHAPTER ✦ ONE

The Unseen Enemy

When I found the lump in my left breast, it looked like nothing more sinister than a slightly raised blue bruise. It wasn't the rounded pea, marble or ping-pong ball all women picture in their wildest nightmares, but just a discoloured ridge, about two inches from the breastbone.

Before I could get up the nerve to prod it, I told myself that, whatever it was ('Now come on, dear Lord, not *that*!'), I must have done it leaning on the ladder to decorate the Christmas tree. That, or it was a pulled muscle, a whack from a bra hook, or a streak of good old healthy dirt. It could be anything, I argued, except a new and alien part of me – the bit you read about, and I write about in the newspapers, but which never happens to us.

I knew from the start I lied. Somehow the dear old familiar boob – suddenly terribly dear to me – looked odd, out of line. To put it crudely, because there's no elegant way of describing a foreign lump, I no longer hung right.

The second I touched the lump, I knew. It was rock-hard, the size of a walnut, and, when I plucked up the courage it took to get a grip on the thing, I could isolate it, like a drawer

I

knob, from the rest of my body. Whatever this thing was inside me, it had a life of its own. And, left to itself, I suspected, a quick death.

The full-length mirror in my shoebox London flat hangs in my bedroom between my teenage son's framed posters of Marilyn Monroe – it's the only space for them, and he relishes the irony. I watched my freezing face age fifteen years in five seconds, and petrify into a Greek tragic mask. On either side of me, Marilyn smiled serenely above her eternal cleavage. Dead at thirty-six, and still a living legend, it struck me she was well out of it. At least she died with her fabled frontage, and everything else, intact, and didn't have this lot to face in her fifties.

By now time, and my heart, must have been standing still for five minutes. Alastair Burnet was still steadily reading the news on my bedroom TV. I would have to cancel Thursday's lunch with him, I thought – illogically wrapping myself in a sheet, and unreasonably yelling aloud at Alastair, my one-time editor and still close friend, 'How can you go on calmly rabbiting when the whole world, or at any rate my world, has just come to an end?'

This was 10.20 p.m., Monday. By 1 p.m. on the following Thursday, at the precise time I would have been ordering a Dover sole in Alastair's favourite Frith Street restaurant, L'Épicure, I was being carved up on the operating table.

Six weeks later, it was Alastair, bless him, who urged me, in a letter, to write all this down: 'Your courage and resilience could be an encouragement to so many people. Though this may sound presumptuous and unfair, it may be that you have been asked to go through an experience of suffering, and thereby a test, so that you can help others. We never know why we're called on to face things, but I do believe there is a meaning to it all.'

I cherish his words, along with a note from my old chum and Fleet Street rival, Jilly Cooper, nudging me: 'What you write about this could be invaluable, with your humour, common sense, and ability to express yourself in a readable way. You're just the right person to do it, but get on with it before you forget exactly how traumatic it was. You don't want to scare people,' she added, 'so your recovery would make a wonderful ending to a book.' Knowing Jilly, I read between the lines, 'For God's sake don't die in chapter three, or you'll do more bloody harm than good!'

Meantime, that black Monday evening, all 'courage and resilience' was now a puddle on the bathroom mat to which I'd moved for a closer examination of the lump in a magnifying mirror. Blown up, the thing looked like Ben Nevis. How could I have missed it before tonight? All right, so I'd never given my breasts the regular, in-depth, ordnance surveys you're supposed to perform past the age of forty. But I had occasionally mauled them about a bit, and they'd always seemed soft and normal.

Only three weeks before, on an assignment in Dubai, I'd swum every morning. Had the lump been visible then, there was no way this now mini-Mount Etna, which seemed to be growing by the minute, would not have shown up through an elasticated swimsuit.

What I tell you now is only my side of my story, and shouldn't alarm women who've found new life in taking HRT (hormone replacement therapy). The fact is that ten days before I found the lump, I'd started on a course of HRT for the first time in what I felt was becoming my rather jaded life.

At fifty-six I was a year younger than Jackie Onassis, a year older than Joan Collins, and born the same year as Elizabeth Taylor. Jackie O, at this time, was driving 'hopelessly in love' twenty-nine-year-old pop millionaire, Michael Jackson, even more than usually whacko. Joan Collins was handling forty-year-old, well-built Bungalow Bill Wiggins like her private property. And Liz Taylor had just miraculously shed five of her thirteen-and-a-half stones and squeezed into what seemed to be a brand new, size eight, ironed-out skin. Like millions of ordinary women, I've never aspired to their big league. But, at exactly their age, why should I feel, as I had for about six months, as if I was dropping clean out of any sort of running?

Besides, Barbara Cartland, who swears by oestrogen, had

just appeared on *Wogan*, at eighty-six, looking like a half-open pink chiffon tea rose. Not much more careworn, dammit, than one of the 460 fluffy blonde virgins on the paperbacks of her best-selling romantic novels. Barbara, who lives in the shade of a pink parasol from April to October, has nagged me for years, 'If you won't stay out of the sun that's going to wrinkle you like an old prune by the time you're sixty-five, at least take oestrogen' – as do she, Taylor, Collins, and, it's rumoured, the tireless Maggie Thatcher and the Queen Mum.

The sun in which I've bathed, like a careless ass, all round the year and the world, has long been my undoing. Even at thirty, I'd begun to weather like a Cornish lobster fisher. But the magical oestrogen in HRT sounded like a much-needed shot in the morale. I was finally pushed into it by Kate O'Mara, the star with the opal Siamese cat's eyes who, as Caress Morrell in *Dynasty*, spends part of the soap opera with her wrists locked in diamond bracelets, and the rest in handcuffs in a Cuban jail. Kate, at forty-eight, looked lithe as an advert for Kit-e-Kat, as she arched herself kittenishly round a BBC canteen chair purring, 'HRT is the greatest treasure of a middle-aged woman's life. It's the elixir, I promise you. These days I feel like a teenager just raring for some handsome billionaire prince to gallop off with me on his white horse.'

Be that as it may, kiss-me-Kate convinced me I'd nothing to lose but the price of this priceless youth elixir at our village Boots.

That HRT was *not* the cause of my breast lump is beyond all doubt. I hadn't been taking it long enough, and, anyway, I was told much later, when I got up the outright courage to ask for it straight, 'You had that lump certainly for months, and probably for years.'

I found this news at once upsetting and strangely consoling. Upsetting, because I hadn't found my walnut when it was a pinhead in its first stages. Consoling, because it precluded that anguished longing for yesterday we all feel in a crisis. It was pointless me whining, 'Let it be six months ago, when my son and I were flying across America, and I was healthy and without a care in the world.' I *hadn't* been flawless on that plane. And knowing now that, even then, my Unseen Enemy was strapped with me in the same seat, somehow gives me more grit to grasp and face it.

There are three expert schools of thought on the lump finding. The surgeon who removed it is convinced its discovery and the ten days' taking of HRT were 'purely coincidental'. My oncologist allowed a 'striking coincidence' in the timing, but stressed, 'One malignant cell can take a very long time doubling, re-doubling, and progressing to the point at which it suddenly becomes a noticeable lump. In your case, that critical moment could have been incidental to taking the HRT.' I wished he hadn't made it sound quite so much like dry rot. My gynaecologist, who had delivered our son by Caesarian section sixteen years before, backs my own belief that 'The oestrogen irritated and inflamed the lump, and chucked it up so you could feel and even see it.' Personally, I'm convinced, and, if right, thankful, that HRT was the underground mole which threw up my hillock and therefore saved my life.

I was thankful for nothing on 14 December 1987, the darkest midnight of my life. Ten days to Christmas, five days to a party we were throwing for fifty people, and three days to my son's homecoming from Eton. How was I going to tell him, 'This year, your mother's really wrecked the icing on the Christmas cake'?

They say the drowning see their past life in a flash. Actually, it was my son's sixteen years I saw. He changed from a five-pound-four-ounces white-shawled bundle to a near-six-feet, gravel-voiced young man with size ten feet, like a fast-forwarded video tape. Occasionally the video frame would freeze, like my very blood, at the thought of leaving him, if what I was convinced I now had meant business.

The fleeting images were in full colour, with stereo sound. His first word – 'car'. His first shrieking blond basin of a hair-cut like Henry V's. First bruise, bloody knee, navy-capped days at kindergarten, first nights at prep school plays. In another, happier full-length mirror than the one in which I was still dumbly staring, I watched him try on his first Eton

5

black frock coat, waistcoat and striped trousers. A penguin trying to scowl like Lord Byron.

I was winding back this mental weepie for another self-indulgent howl, when it hit me what he'd have said, had he been in his next-door bedroom, gruesomely papered with heavy metal posters, and shaking with wall-to-wall sound . . .

'For God's sake, Mum, I've found dozens of lumps all over me at school. You're not dead yet!'

2 a.m. By now my husband would be asleep, out of phone-shot, in the family home in Kent. In any case, why wake him to share my new burden when there was nothing he could do but work himself into a frenzy? By 5 a.m., my mind, and my M & S nightie, were in tattered shreds. I'd spent the sleepless night tearing it and my body apart, convincing myself *it* wasn't there.

Wouldn't it just have to be a Tuesday, the day on which I've written my column in the *Express* for fifteen years? I fervently believe if you're well-paid, well-televised, and well-plastered across the country's billboards, you've a duty to deliver the goods. The only day I hadn't come up with them I was giving birth. The next week, still in hospital, I wrote my column, then in the *Daily Mail*, with my right hand, while I bottle-fed the baby with my left. If he has ink in his blood, it's probably literal.

The column itself has always been an agonizing birth. Labour starts when two alarm clocks knock me out of bed at 5 a.m., and finishes around 4 p.m., when I'm wrung dry.

So, at first light, as usual, I dragged myself downstairs. 'Don't look, and you won't see the lump. Don't feel a thing, and it will have gone away . . .' I stuck it out, in a bright red towelling bath robe, a reminder of a jolly family holiday in Marbella, until halfway through my coffee. Then I felt for the lump which would, of course, have miraculously vanished.

It was there, large as life, and death.

I rang my mother, who had had a breast cancer operation herself, at seventy-six, three years before. 'Ma, what was your lump like?' 'At the side, like a marble,' she said. 'I told you, I found it in the bath. Why?'

6

'Well, I'm sure it's nothing,' I lied. 'But I've found this hard lump in my breast.'

My mother is all Yorkshire common sense, right down to her considerable backbone. A frail but fearless Yorkshire terrier of a woman who at the time didn't even tell me she had cancer. She'd gone in for her lumpectomy the day I was leaving for an assignment in Kenya. At home, I ring her daily. Abroad, I only send cards, a habit on which she'd counted to hide her secret.

When I rang from Heathrow, as my flight was being called, she said, 'Good luck – have a great time!' Three weeks later, already in radiotherapy, she dismissed her ordeal: 'What would you have done if I'd told you? Got off the flight and fallen down on the job to drive to Hull and sit staring at me? Don't be daft!'

Now she said, 'It'll be nothing, but I should have it looked at right away.' I could hear in her voice that 'Well, we'll see' tone I remembered from toddlerhood. I think Mother knew, in her anxious heart, that this time her little fifty-six-year-old daughter wasn't going to have things all her own way.

I rang my husband of twenty-four years. 'I've found this lump in my breast, and I think it's cancer,' I said. 'Geoff, I'm terrified.' There was a pause.

'So am I,' said the voice, twenty-nine miles away. It was a closer, more cherishable remark than 'I love you' or 'Chin up'.

I backed my beautiful 4.2 Jaguar out of my yuppie Wapping flat – the sweet fruit of thirty-one hard years in journalism – and drove down to Fleet Street. I read the papers with one eye on the clock for the 8 a.m. arrival of the *Express*'s first aid department. A newspaper's medical staff deals with real, split-second emergencies. Only the previous week, one of our nurses had shinned up a dangerous piece of machinery, grabbed a printworker's severed finger-end with one hand and the man with the other, and dashed with them to Charing Cross hospital to be re-stitched.

They would laugh off my lump as nothing but a lost night's sleep. Of course they would.

'Sit up very straight,' said our Scottish Sister. I'd only fumbled with the lump standing, or lying down. Straight-backed, there was no getting round it. The thing was a boulder.

'Stop it, pull yourself together, it could be a cyst or a bit of fatty tissue,' snapped Sister, with all the controlled strength she'd once used to yank six poisonous spines from my foot, left in from standing on something disgusting on a job in Indonesia. 'But this has to be looked into right away. What do you want to do?'

'Out, out!' I shrieked, like Lady Macbeth with her damned spot.

'All right – I'll make you a lunchtime appointment with a private clinic, but it'll be expensive,' she said.

No expense spared. No waiting, I had to know *now*. Weeks later, sitting in a line of well-scuffed chairs outside our local hospital's radiotherapy department, in a patient queue of NHS cancer sufferers who had no choice but to wait, I was to feel ashamed of my moment of madness and Mammon. But at the time I would have mortgaged my soul for an assurance that they could save my life.

In the ten years she'd worked for me, since she was nineteen, my secretary, Nicola Janson, had always arrived before, or on the bleep of 10 a.m. National morning newspapers work from 10 a.m. until they hit the street, never boring nine to five. On black Tuesdays, Nicky used to find me staring into space. This morning she knew even halfway through the door that I was seeing something worse than just blank paper.

When I told her, she turned white as the sheet on which I hadn't typed a single word. We both cried, then laughed at ourselves because 'Of course it'll turn out to be nothing,' and hugged each other as we had at moments of crisis, through a decade of my Fleet Street triumphs and my fair smattering of disasters.

Somehow, by 6 p.m. – two hours late – I was to hack out some sort of a dazed Page 9, between rushing round London for consultations and X-rays. In print next morning, my words had all the spark of a fused word processor, and our theatre critic Maureen Paton, had had to fill a nasty hole down the side of my page.

But at the end of that hideous day, I had at least done my job. Just as I'd done, nineteen years previously, when my mother rang me, in the middle of my column for the *Daily Sketch*, to tell me my beloved father had finally died of lung cancer. Then, I finished the column for him, as he would have expected of me. Now, I had to prove myself to myself, or go under before the fight had even begun.

Whenever things got hopelessly snarled up, Nicky and I had a running gag: 'Oh well, it can't be worse than Prince William Day.' Even after a working lifetime in journalism, you can occasionally, for no apparent reason, lose your head, drift, thread and nerve on a big story. I lost the lot on the Duke and Duchess of York's wedding day.

It was a hefty responsibility to have the *Express*'s single precious ticket to a superb seat in Westminster Abbey. I was only a diamond's throw from the royals, and so near Prince Philip I sweated when our eyes locked, since it's well known in Fleet Street and Buck House that he's never forgiven me for describing him on his sixty-fifth birthday as 'a snappish OAP with a temper like an arthritic corgi'.

Add to this, in the near-hysterical run-up to the most trumpeted event of the year, I'd done far too much research. What I didn't know about Andrew and Fergie – every published and televised word either had breathed, and every nook, cranny and flower in the abbey – wasn't worth knowing. I couldn't have fitted all I knew into the Archbishop of Canterbury's Bible, let alone the *Express*'s front page, into which I was hell-bent on cramming it.

Back at the excited office – with one eye on the TV you're obliged to watch in case Buck House's balcony collapses, under the weight of all those royals, while you're still warbling on about the wedding ceremony – I didn't know where to begin on my endless notes. I started on Fergie's dress, with its diamante A's and anchors, then scrapped it. Picked instead on her coronet of wild flowers, then ditched those.

My golden words, chiming like wedding bells, should have hit the editor's desk at the latest by 5 p.m. At 5.30., I was still disastrously entangled in Fergie's eighteen-foot train and tumbling red hair, and hadn't written an intelligible word.

At 6 p.m., poor Nicky – now gamely lying 'She'll be finished any minute,' on two phones to seven people – was the colour of the *Express*'s still-empty front page. In all our working lives, we'd never had a row. Now I thought she was going to hit me.

'I don't give a damn what you write, but write something!' she shouted. Normally she never swore. 'Pretend you're a young reporter back on the *Sheffield Telegraph*, when you *daren't* have kept them waiting, and put down the first bloody thing that comes into your head!'

I stopped short, as if slapped, gasped for air, and typed . . .

There were 30,000 flowers in the abbey, along with history's most blooming royal bride. But it was Sweet William's day. The four-year-old future king blossomed wickedly.

He stuck out his tongue, like a surplus rose, at the blushing bridesmaids. With his sailor hat on the back of his saucy head, he steered the little girls down the aisle like a fleet of taffeta tugs.

Then Just William discovered that his hatband was elastic. He snapped it. He flipped it. He poked it in his eye. Then he rammed it into his mouth, loop by loop, like spaghetti . . .

Less than half an hour, and 1000 words later, I ended with . . .

Behind the altar, the throne which William V will ascend at his Coronation stood in dusty silence. On the day he is crowned, he will not remember the four-year-old's little imperfections which made this Royal Wedding the perfect day.

But the family album will never let him forget . . .

The readers, God bless 'em, loved it. Even I have to say it flowed so smoothly you couldn't see the joins. Let alone that I had so nearly cracked.

Now, inwardly falling apart, I glanced for the umpteenth time at the clock, and told Nicky, 'If I've got to be at that clinic by noon I'll have to leave now.'

'This is worse than Prince William Day,' she said. 'I'll come with you.' It nearly choked me to watch her automatically reach for her spiral notebook in which, un-asked, she'd always done the unpaid job of sorting out my messy private life. Whatever the news, she was going to take a note.

Outside, what little self-control I had left over my now total panic was switched off by London's Christmas lights. I hated their maddeningly cheerful glitter, the packed, good-natured traffic. Oxford Street was a screaming, laughing, rip-roaring roller coaster, still going round and round while my little world might be about to lurch to a stop. There's nothing grimmer, I discovered in the taxi on the way to finding out my fate, than watching other people's on-going lives race by your only precious life which could be in the balance.

And why did they all look so worried? They weren't going to be X-rayed for breast cancer. They were normal and healthy, with nothing to fear from what they might see on a screen, except another night's lousy TV. Those lump-free folk were panicking about nothing but how to cram their presents, their parties, their unwritten cards, into the alarmingly little time left until Christmas.

But only twenty-four hours ago hadn't I been frantic about just the same foolish things? God, how I'd griped about my weary working woman's load! What I'd give now to have only my happy heap of half-finished Christmas to carry, instead of this hard lump of terror!

We were cruising round the back of John Lewis's, with £4.20 on the clock. Any minute, I'd tap on the window, fling the driver a jovial fiver, give Nicky the slip, dive into Lewis's, blue every last penny in my bank account, plus a £1,000 overdraft for luck, and then I'd go home. I'd con the family it was a false alarm, and wipe the whole ugly picture from my mind. Over Christmas, I'd eat, drink, and be merry, for tomorrow. . . .

The private clinic was off Harley Street, but not far enough off for financial comfort. It was hushed, plushed, and, I calculated from the price of the wall-to-wall everything, fabulously expensive. Nobody here had climbed up to decorate their Christmas tree on a ladder like the one I still vaguely hoped could have caused my lumpy bruise. Theirs was all of £1,000-worth, fully dressed, and straight from Harrods' floor show. By the time I'd sunk into a gold leather armchair and picked up *Country Life* from one of the crystal-topped tables, spattered like ritzy raindrops on the gold carpet, I'd mentally spent a term's Eton fees.

The Arab cancer specialist was hawkishly handsome, forty-ish, and, under jollier circumstances, a Red Shadow any woman would have relished falling across her path. Trying to touch me, he couldn't understand why I was shying like a virgin from Rudolf Valentino's grasp. 'You're terrified, aren't you?' he marvelled. 'I've never seen anyone so frightened in my life.'

'Haven't I seen you before, Mrs Nash?' he asked, struggling to get more of a grip on me than I could get on myself. 'It's Jean Rook in the paper, and on telly, but don't believe all that Fearless, Formidable, Forthright First Lady of Fleet Street you've read about me,' I said. 'I've just found out that I'm a totally cowardly lioness, and a rotten sham.'

'Everyone is about cancer,' he said gently. 'Some people just show it more.'

He eventually gave me the once, then the twice-over. And some hope. 'Yes, there's a lump all right, but it seems to be quite "loose" and not impacted in the breast. Probably mastitis. I'll send you up the road for a mammogram, and if you bring back the X-rays I'll look at them on the spot.'

'Up the road' actually *was* Harley Street. Another genuine Georgian door, opening on to a wall-lit, chandeliered, silk-walled film set of a waiting room.

By this time, my tugged-about breast was sore, swollen, and the lump was the Rock of Gibraltar. And it hurt like hell.

This cheered me wildly, since, as every lay fool has read, breast cancer doesn't hurt until it's actually terminating you. And surely it doesn't grow this quickly? You could virtually see me evolving like something out of Disney's *Fantasia*. My boob was a crimson Christmas party balloon. Surely it wouldn't fit inside the Cartier-like glass case into which it had to be squeezed to be X-rayed? They eventually managed, but the pain was murderous.

Back at the clinic, half an hour and another fifty pounds later – private health care doesn't hang about – the surgeon examining my X-rays announced, 'I can see nothing carcinomatoid here, so I'll put you on antibiotics until Thursday.' It was a Christmas carol to my ears. Nicky and I actually sang one in the taxi. Regent Street glittered above and around us. I outsparkled it. I didn't even care that the pain in my chest was intermittently throbbing like the bright red bulbs flashing around Piccadilly Circus.

At 6.15 p.m., just as I was leaving the office, the phone rang. 'It's Mr X from the clinic. Look, the radiographer has had a look at your mammogram, and if the lump hasn't gone down by Thursday we'll do a biopsy as soon as possible, just to be on the safe side.'

I froze like an icicle, as the axe fell again on my Yule log, and, once again, my cheery lights were blotted out. By now, my agonized husband and mother were trying to keep track of my yo-yo-ing telephone reports. Up, down, back up, back down.

By Thursday, I was determined that the lump would have shrunk like a sock. It hadn't.

'It's smaller, but it's still there. When can we do the biopsy?' asked the Arab surgeon, calm-eyed as a statue of Rameses II.

'When can you?' I said.

'Today,' he said.

'Monday,' I hedged, honestly less in fear than traumatized by the thought of putting off fifty party people at a day's notice. He said he was going to Jordan on Monday, for two weeks, but could refer me to someone else.

Better the devil you're beginning to know, and I liked and

trusted the man. 'I could do it tonight at the Wellington hospital, and you could stay over, or at lunchtime at the Princess Grace, so you could go home in the evening.'

The cost of the cut? 'If you stay overnight at the Wellington, it comes to a thousand pounds all in,' he said.

For only one hell of a night? No wonder egg-stained Edwina Currie had suggested: 'Put off decorating a room, and you could afford private health care.' At these prices, I could redecorate the Dorchester. I'd interviewed Princess Grace years ago, and liked her. I would settle for a lunchtime £600-worth at her place.

The very young nurse who checked me in was more Liverpudlian than Ringo Starr. 'I'm sure it'll be all right, pet, and I'll be there when you come round to tell you what happened.' She was about to leave me alone, with my teeth-chattering thoughts, to strip right down to my contact lenses.

The hospital intercom was playing carols – high, piping choirboys' voices that conjured up flaring candles, and soaring stone. They flashed me back to the previous Sunday's carol concert in Eton College chapel. 'Don't worry, pet, I'll change the tape,' the little nurse read my face. 'But we've only got Ella Fitzgerald.'

Anything but Bing Crosby's 'White Christmas' would do.

The Red Shadow surgeon swept through my cubicle curtains. To pass the anaesthetist's time, we chatted about my coverage of Charles and Diana's tour of the Gulf. For at least a few minutes, my thoughts galloped far away on the white steeds surrounding the Arabian Nights feast the Saudis had spread for us in the desert outside Riyad. It seemed many crescent moons ago since I'd walked with the royals over 284 priceless Persian carpets, spread on the sand, and eaten exotica off solid gold platters, while we watched a parade of spotless, actually shampooed, pale cream camels.

A killing thought slashed through me. 'What if this turns out to be malignant – I mean what will you do?' I said.

'Biopsy it, wake you up, tell you all, make a further appointment for surgery, and take it from there,' he said.

No chance. Never. Only right *now*. Knowing my family

would feel as I did, I asked if I could sign anything authorizing him to do anything, right there on the table.

'Anything?' he queried.

'Yes, even if it means waking up and finding I've lost the lot. But don't bring me round to tell me I've got to go back under, or you'll never see me again.'

All my life, until now, I'd been boisterously healthy. I'd suffered nothing but the odd February cold, the Caesarian for toxaemia, and my tonsils out, at eight.

Ridiculously out of date, I expected the long Dr Kildare trolley ride to the theatre, the brilliant arc lights, the mask, and the five-four-three-two-one countdown to those winking stars before the deep dark night. So why was this pleasant guy, in a room no bigger than my kitchen, fiddling with my right hand? I felt everything slipping. I thought of my loved ones, watching their clocks: 'It'll only take twenty minutes, I'll call you.'

If this goes wrong, I mused dreamily, I wonder if they'll hold my memorial in the journalists' Fleet Street church, St Bride's? Or in St Paul's? It would be bound to be St Paul's. After all, I was – still am – the First Lady of Fleet Street. . . .

CHAPTER ✦ TWO

Fledgling First Lady

I didn't aim, from pramhood, to grow up into 'Britain's bitchiest, best-known, loved, and loathed woman journalist'.

When I was a girl in Hull, my Lincolnshire father hoped I would be a barrister. My Yorkshire mother wanted me to be an English teacher. I burned to play Lady Macbeth at Stratford. But, like many a luscious northern lass, I was big-boobed, big-bottomed, short-waisted, and, even as a five-feet-seven-and-a-half-inch teenager, weighed thirteen stones. I could see myself as a stage-shaking Lady Macbeth, the demon queen plucking her mighty nipple from her offspring's boneless gums. But, as a fourteen-year-old Juliet, I would have broken the balcony.

At eighteen, I sadly accepted that I was the wrong size and shape to be a great, all-round actress. Ironically, that great, physically all-round, big-boobed, bottomed and short-waisted actress, Dame Judi Dench, has since proved me wrong. I was awestruck watching Judi who, offstage, can look like a chunky home-knitted jumper, give her crowning performance at the National Theatre, in 1987, as the definitively sinuous, sex-soaked Cleopatra. I was proud that this fellow county-woman, whom I first saw as a nineteen-year-old Virgin Mary in the York Miracle Plays, had realized the immortal longings for applause we both must have felt, as contemporary teenagers born a few miles apart.

As a youngster, fame was not just my spur. My consuming ambition slashed me to ribbons even as a fat kid in plaits. Whatever I was going to be, it had to be big. I always saw my name in lights. If the actual light bulbs failed me, I've at least seen it in the biggest, boldest type ever used on a Fleet Street by-line.

How short on modesty? Totally. When you've typed your fingers to the bone for thirty-two years, you expect all the accolades you can grab. But I'm not as megalomaniacal as my critics like to believe. Newspaper legend has it that I crowned myself the First Lady of Fleet Street on my first morning on the *Daily Express*. If I'd thought of it, I might have. Certainly *Private Eye* and every TV chat show host who's interviewed me insists that my triumphal entry into the Black Lubianka, as the *Express* is nicknamed, was as arrogant as Nancy Reagan's take-over of the White House.

Not only was I, and am I, the highest paid woman in Fleet Street, but it's rumoured I reckon I own it. Now that Fleet Street's been sold, and the *Express* has moved across the river, I'll doubtless be renamed the Witch of Wapping.

In fact, I was dubbed Fleet Street's First Lady by a hard-selling *Express* deputy editor, four days before I even joined the paper, in 1972. In bed one morning, my husband read out, 'SHE'S FRANK, FORTHRIGHT, FORMIDABLE, FEARLESS AND INFURIATING! SHE IS THE FIRST LADY OF FLEET STREET!! YOU CAN'T AFFORD TO MISS HER!!!'

'By God, she must be good,' I said. 'Whatever paper's that?'

'It's the *Daily Express*, and you'd better be good, because she's you, you chump,' my husband yawned and turned to the sports pages.

As my *Sheffield Telegraph* mentor, who taught me from scratch, nothing I've written ever had a huge impact on

Geoff. Apart from a note I once taped to the fridge: 'Sorry, gone to China, back in a month.'

Next day, the *Express*'s living legendary cartoonist, Giles, snatched up the title when one of his murderous, bun-shaped babies appeared on the front page, waving a placard, 'Down With Women's Lib! Fire the First Lady of Fleet Street Before She Starts!' Giles, who sets his real life hearthrug of a dog on people who let slip his age (seventy-two) will thump me for telling you I cut out his cartoons as a schoolgirl, and that one of the perks of joining the *Express* was the thrill of shaking the hand that shaped Grandma. To be publicly pilloried by the Old Master was such instant stardom in itself, my mother nearly cried with excitement. Giles has poked pen, paintbrush, and so much unflagging fun at me, over sixteen years, my walls are now hung with insults far more valuable to me than the £3,000 an original Giles cartoon fetches at auction. My pet affront is a killer rook, with a half-eaten politician in its beak, captioned: 'Anyone Jean Rook Doesn't Like.'

Within weeks, the 'First Ladyship' was indelibly inked on me. I can't swear who re-titled me The First Bitch of Fleet Street on live television. Michael Parkinson said it was Russell Harty, who assured me it was Terry Wogan, who claims it was Michael Parkinson. Actually, of all unlikely assassins, I think it was Derek Nimmo during a terse moment on his seventies chat show.

I'd made the mistake of thinking that, since he's played so many vicars, Nimmo's programme would be polite as a rectory tea party. Five seconds into the interview, he made a cucumber sandwich of me with ungodly sarcasm. *The Times*' TV critic was so stunned by our brief but bloody encounter, he wrote: 'Derek Nimmo's attempted crucifixion of Jean Rook was like watching a budgerigar trying to savage a vulture.'

If it was Nimmo who stuck me with 'The First Bitch', I can only bless him for giving my column bigger, sharper teeth in the public view. You either really like or absolutely lump my column. Addicts often ask me if I began to be 'cutting' the moment I cut my teeth. Truthfully, I've never been acerbic for acid's sake. If a columnist aggressively sits down at a typewriter with the attitude, 'This morning I'll rough up the royals and spark off sacks of furious letters,' readers see through the ploy, feel patronized, and don't rise to the bait.

I've always said what I think, forcefully and, I hope, amusingly, at the given moment. Hundreds who feel as I do write back. The rest, who wouldn't deign to light the Aga with Rook's rubbish, write in even sooner. My heftiest mail bag was a thousand letters in forty-eight hours, for calling Mrs Mary Whitehouse 'a whited sepulchre who hands out black marks to programmes she doesn't watch through her half-closed fingers'. Six agreed with me, 994 wanted me sacked, and the *Express*'s switchboard was blocked for four hours.

Being Yorkshire is a bonus. All Yorkshire folk call a spade a shovel and, when roused, dig the graves of people who irritate them. One of the few memorable remarks made by Roy Hattersley is his comment, in his autobiography, *Goodbye to Yorkshire*, that all Yorkshire people are born winners who would as soon throw themselves off Flamborough Head as lose even a brass band contest. This is why Harvey Smith rides at life like an eight-foot wall, Geoff Boycott clouts it for six, and Arthur Scargill would call his own shadow out on strike.

I just write it all down. Years ago, when I wrote, 'Our Queen needs her eyebrows plucking', I was stunned by the eyebrows it raised round the world to which my column is widely syndicated. And genuinely perplexed by the maddened mobs who attacked me, 'How dare you, you bitch – our Queen does a wonderful job!' Our Queen does, has, and always will do a wonderful job. She still needs her privet hedge eyebrows plucking.

I'm often asked if I'm a royalist. Indubitably and fiercely. Despite Prince Edward, who nearly KO'd the entire monarchy by making a motley fool of himself and his family on *It's a Knockout*, our royalty is our finest showcase, and we should hang on to every thread of the old ermine. But it's not a glass case, in which its members should be breathlessly viewed from a distance, like the crown jewels. If the royals, particularly the younger set, make a sketch of themselves by behaving more like 'one of us' even than one of us, why not note it? Or, as I only asked at the end of the Duchess of York's fashionably tasteless '88 tour of Hollywood, 'Who, in wardrobe, let the disastrous Duchess loose at a charity dinner in those red-ruched Odeon cinema curtains that looked about to part on Joan Crawford?'

I'm asked, too, if my column comes naturally to me? The sentiment, in a flash. Expressing it in readable form can take mere heady minutes when your mind is up and ticking, or tedious, sweating hours when it's not, and every word has to be dragged out with pliers.

But, on the whole, I find no great difficulty in commenting, to take one example, on dithering Dr Robert Runcie's handing over of £1,200 of Church funds to unchecked conmen who persuaded him that they could release his envoy, Terry Waite. To an ordinary soul like me, it seems the most logical thing on earth to inquire,

> On Doomsday, when they separate the sheep from the goats, where will they put that ineffectual old bleater, the Archbishop of Canterbury? Dr Runcie isn't good enough. Or, if he's good enough in the sight of Heaven, he's no damned use down here.

Professional Yorkshire folk, like Parky, who's made a pile out of his Barnsley slag heaps, are proud of telling how they made it all from nowt, pulled themselves out of the muck by their boot laces, and coined their own brass. I admit I didn't have to. My father was a successful self-made consultant engineer who had left Boston, Lincs, with thirty pounds, stacks of ambition, and a roll of wallpaper with which he personally DIY'd the first of his several north-of-England offices. He went on to earn local fame, and, if not fortune, a first-class living.

My mother, sixteen years his junior, was a sweetly pretty usherette at the now defunct Tivoli Variety Theatre, Hull. The night they met, my father was sporting a wire-wheeled car, a Dalmatian dog, spats, and enough ready cash to buy the end seat on row H at the Tivoli for the next three months when my mother, already engaged to somebody else, spurned his very rapid advances. He sat out twelve performances of *Lilac Time* before mother, out of stunned curiosity, agreed to go out with him. Four months later they were married, and welded the gap between Yorks and Lincs, forty years before the building of the Humber Bridge.

We moved from Hull after the first year of World War II. My father, who had lied his way, at 17, into World War I, and had half his stomach shot away at the battle of the Somme, was devastated when they turned him down for active service, at forty-five, in 1939, and shelved him, as an Army captain with the Ministry of War Transport, stationed at York. All I remember of the Hull blitz was the underside of our oak dining table, as we had no snazzy Anderson shelter. Any other woman but my stolid little mother would have wailed like the nightly sirens, about the conditions in bombed and battered Hull, but she never complained, or explained to my father when he rang from nearby, untouched York.

One weekend father came home on leave and flung wide the front door to listen to the fascinating shriek of the air-raid warnings York didn't have. It was a Friday night when Hitler blasted father from his shattered front door and into the back pantry. On Monday, father got things moving at the same speed with which he'd hurtled through the house. By Thursday we were evacuated, lock, stock and dining table, to Westerdale, a small village nineteen miles inland from Whitby, in the bleak middle of the North Yorkshire moors.

When my essentially urban mother first saw Westerdale Hall, now a youth hostel, with its twin-turreted towers, three winding staircases, twenty bedrooms, stone passages and secret panels, she lifted up her voice, even on the stately doorstep, and wept. After discovering rats in the cellar, bats in the belfry, and Mickey-size mice thoughout, she threatened divorce. We had no electricity, no heating, Victorian oil lamps, and paraffin cooking in our reputedly haunted house, in which a pair of star-crossed lovers were said to have hurled themselves from a turret. My mother had a bitter theory that they died of frostbite first.

My four years at Westerdale, as a wildly imaginative, only and lonely child, were the happiest of my life. I believe I was put down for Roedean soon after birth; but when I howled that I didn't want to go, my mother shrieked that there was a war on, the forties excuse for wriggling out of anything you didn't fancy, my father flung up his tied hands and sent me to the village school. The day I won Westerdale's first scholarship to Whitby County School in seventeen years – not particularly bright of me after my Hull Froebel education – the village rang out the great news on its three church bells.

I admit I had a lovely, windswept, carefree moorland war, riding on top of the outdoor world I loved, on my bike in summer, and in winter on horseback through the vast snows which sometimes even trapped us by the log fire for weeks I never wanted to end.

At the end of the war, we slunk back, like the lucky cowards I suppose we were, to what was left of poor old bomb-blasted Hull. I slogged on at Malet Lambert Grammar School, never getting less than ninety-two per cent in English – I don't expect my regular readers to believe that – and never more than twelve per cent in maths. Only because, as my maths master sarcastically summed it up, 'It was the easiest paper in fifteen years, and even then you didn't deserve it,' I scraped the obligatory university entrance maths O level.

I was thrilled to get interviews for Oxford and Cambridge, and, at the time, spirit-broken to get into neither. With ten O levels, nine of them grade ones, and four distinctive A levels, I suspected I lost out because I came from the 'wrong', unsung, co-ed grammar school. In my day, female Oxbridge was constrictedly blue stocking, and fearfully snooty. It's ironic that now, nearly forty years on, your best chance of cracking Oxford is to be a comprehensive pinkish Trot.

Looking back, it was fate that prevented me becoming a possible academic dreamer among the spires. The University of London had much to offer, best of all London at your fingertips, with its theatres, crazy clubs, and the then just emerging King's Road, Chelsea.

Also at my fingertips were men. Having no great looks, but, by now, a great if overweight shape, in the busty fifties mould, I set out to further my co-education by dating as many as I could cram into seven nights a week, and Sunday afternoon off lectures.

Logistically, I'd severely restricted my love life by landing a place at all-female Bedford College, a beautiful building superbly planted in Regent's Park. But there were ways and means of wrought-iron-gate-crashing, after curfew, and I was slim enough now to crawl in through the back kitchen window. I had to teach these valuable lessons in Life to the rest of my year, most of whom had come virginally fresh from Roedean and Cheltenham Ladies' College in the days when such genuine ladies were ignorant about men. Half of them had only spoken to their brothers.

My co-education thrilled and shocked them. Their accents, after my war years on the moors, riveted me. On my first morning someone asked me to 'pars the sawlt'. As one who'd always 'passt the solt', I was entranced. Immediately, I began to take 'barths', and stroll the primrose 'parths' of my youth practising a's so long, it took hours to drawl out a sentence.

Bedford flashed by, all too quickly, in a permanent summer haze of tennis, rowing at five in an eight on the Thames, romantic park picnics, and oceans of midnight oil.

I dipped the First my disappointed tutors had me marked down for, but squeezed a decent Upper Second. I was raring to get to grips with 'real life' when father flung a spanner in the works by promising me a car if I would press on for a Master's degree in English. Unlike Oxbridge, London won't flog you an MA. I'd a choice between 'The Impact of T. S. Eliot on the English Drama of His Time', and losing my chance of a small, second-hand Ford.

My father, as ever, was wise. I've never regretted even a dull moment of learning to discipline myself to work alone. But working alone for eighteen months on my thesis, in the Reading Room of the British Museum, slammed all doors on any fleeting thoughts I might have had, as fleetingly I did, of entering the groves of academe, and becoming the English mistress mother dreamed of.

Eight hours a day in the British Museum is a killer, unless you're a mummy. My only light and fanciful relief was a trip to the dusty music library to hold hands with a gorgeous, curly-haired Byron called Malcolm Bradbury. He was forever working on a novel called *Eating People is Wrong*. I thought this the daftest, non-selling title until it made him famous, years later, and I read it serialized in one of the Sunday heavies.

By now, the writing was on the wall of my future career. I was the first woman to edit the university newspaper, *Sennet*, and the ink was seeping into my blood.

When I applied for a non-paid vacation job on my home town's then tatty rag, the *Hull Daily Mail*, their news editor ripped up my future with, 'You're far too old [I was twenty-five], you've spent far too much time on education you'll never need, and I can tell you now, you haven't a cat in hell's chance of getting to Fleet Street.'

At that moment, I knew I'd make Fleet Street if I had to crawl from the Strand to Saint Paul's in gutters running with my own blood. I wrote to the *Sunday Times* and the *Observer* that I was God's gift to them, and, with their advice, landed a place on the graduate trainee scheme run by the *Sheffield Telegraph*.

Telling my parents was tricky. They couldn't see a fat future in £7 8s 9d a week, and couldn't I do more with what even I was beginning to think was my over-education? Telling my Bedford tutor, Professor Una Ellis Fermor, was traumatic, particularly since she believed she was the reincarnation of Christopher Marlowe, and had a mind sharper than the knife that stabbed him.

She stared at me as if the *Sheffield Telegraph* was Mars. 'You could have been a great English teacher at one of our finest schools!' she thundered, as the Lear-like storm of her disapproval, and genuine shock, broke over her. Then her face cleared. 'Ah well, my dear,' she said, 'perhaps you're doing the right thing if it's what you really want. It would be terrible to wake up at the top of the tree, at forty-five, to realize you'd climbed the wrong tree.' It's a remark I've carried next to my heart all the long climb to today, and shall carry to the end.

The *Sheffield Telegraph*, at that time housed in a white latrine building which had yellowed like a decayed tooth, promised to be hell, and didn't disappoint. My news editor, Ernest Taylor, unaffectionately known as the Barnsley Bull, was the devil unhung. In those days, few provincial journalists were graduates. Having left school at fourteen, Ernest wasn't going to waste more time on me than I'd already wasted 'learning all that poetry and not a bloody word of shorthand'.

Ernest had what we call in Yorkshire a 'wall eye' – milky, out of kilter, like one of those Ilkley Moor sheepdogs that can't look straight at you. He never looked anywhere near me for the three weeks I sat behind the office's worst, all but toothless typewriter, mourning, 'This way, I'll never be Marjorie Proops.' Since Marje never reveals her age, she'll write me off for this, but it's said with the deepest admiration for her deserved professional longevity.

One magic night, Ernest got stuck with me. The drama critic was off sick, six hundred local amateurs were staging an epic production of *The Life of Christ* in Bradford, I'd been 't't University', and more to the point, I had a little car. The deputy news editor, Geoff Nash, said he would go along for what I suspected was immoral support. As it turned out, he was the *Life of Christ*'s salvation, and mine.

Bradford's view of Christ's life was endless. Finally Geoff took me to a private room he'd hired in a pub, plopped me in front of a phone, and said he'd be back in half an hour for the 'copy'.

Only God knows how I struggled that night to write a piece on the life of His Son. I had no finger nails left, and no words, when Geoff turned up, on the stroke of the time I was to deliver, like Faust's Mephistopheles. 'What do you mean you haven't written anything?' he roared. 'You're not writing essays now, you're working for a morning paper. Unless you want this great career of yours to end now, this minute, you'll pick up the phone and dictate five hundred words on what you've just seen to the woman with a typewriter at the other end. She's called a copy taker.'

'What'll I say to the copy taker?' I whimpered. 'Tell her your name's Jean Rook, and, the way things are going, she can forget it,' he sighed.

'Speak up, what's your catchline?' snapped the copy taker. Catchline? 'What's your story about, in one word?'

'Christ.'

'I beg your pardon?'

'Our Lord,' I said.

'Oh, I see,' she breathed very slowly. 'Well, I'm ready.'

I wasn't, but in sheer hysteria I bawled into the phone, 'Jerusalem was builded last night among the dark, satanic mills of the West Riding's woollen industry . . .' and never drew breath for another eight hundred appalling words. As the boy was pushing the paper through my letter box next morning, I was breathlessly pulling it out the other side. Every word, which in mystical print now looked golden, was at the foot of the front page, and so was my name. It was small, tentative, but it was my first by-line.

I didn't care which way Ernest's eye was swivelling as I strode into the office, on air. 'You gave me a by-line, Mr Taylor,' I said, still clutching the paper I'd read and re-read into ribbons.

'We had to, love,' he replied wearily. 'Your stuff was that bloody clever nobody else here could understand a word of it.'

Ernest decided it was worth his while to teach me a real thing or two about journalism. He dished me out the lousiest jobs – Co-op fashion shows, local dog shows, late night check-calls round the hospitals and the mortuary. 'What do you mean they won't let you see the body, love? You haven't really asked them? Oh, for Christ's sake come back here where you can do less damage!'

With a face as expressionless as a Yorkshire stone wall, he read my first murder report. 'As the woman's husband, who had brutally knifed her in the bathroom only seconds before, tore down the stairs to escape, great gouts of her innocent blood, splashed on the hall wallpaper, cried out "murder!"' Ernest knifed me with a look, slashed out my Gothic master-piece, and wrote, 'A man is helping police with their inquiries'.

For weary weeks he made me check and re-check my facts, write and rewrite my stories. Had I got their full names, ages, occupations, addresses, exact quotes? He sent me back to Attercliffe, not the leafiest corner of Sheffield, seven times, the seventh time to check the colour of the house-owner's eyes.

'You'll not forget in future, love.' Never, until hell freezes. The first time I interviewed Maggie Thatcher, twenty years later, I wrote down 'blue-grey eyes' halfway across the room. Even now, I'm still a dab hand at:

> Mrs Sandra Smith, twenty-seven, blonde-haired, blue-eyed mother of Jason, six, and Sharon, four, told me last night at their three-bedroomed semi-detached home at 24, Wood-pecker Crescent, Rotherham, Yorks, that her twenty-nine-year-old unemployed former bricklayer husband, Tom, had admitted his torrid six-month affair with twenty-two-year-old Barnsley night club stripper, Mary Jones, known to clients of the notorious Barnsley Belle Bottom Club as 'Tassel Tossing Tessa'. Mrs Smith said OPEN QUOTES He is a cheating bastard, and she's welcome to him CLOSE QUOTES. . . .

Looking back over thirty-two years at my hammering from long-dead Ernest, I owe him for what he knocked into me. I've often steadied myself, among 500 rival journalists, and armies of TV crews on a royal tour, with, 'You know what to look for, love, and it's only another job.'

Just as Ernest had me trained to sheepdog perfection, the girl who wrote the *Sheffield Telegraph*'s weekly column, 'Roundabout', left to be married, and I was offered her space. The editor, Bill Lyth, was adamant that I took it. Ernest was rock-solid that I shouldn't. 'There's no opening for women columnists at the top, stick to news reporting.' (I've often hoped Ernest's looked down to see the massive openings I dug for a whole new genre of women columnists.) I was twisted

into a Gordian knot of indecision when Geoff cut through it.
'Forget news. You're only a competent reporter, but you could
be a great feature writer. Times are changing for women.
Grab your chance.'

I was now relying heavily on Geoff, professionally and
socially. Working 2 to 10 p.m. on a provincial paper may be
the School of Life, but it was barren after my man-filled days
at university. I often told Geoff I fell for him because the only
other men I met were members of Sheffield City Council.

My 'Roundabout' column spun merrily with the *ST* readers,
and began to fan out into a wider orbit. Shelved in Sheffield,
I dreamed that every Fleet Street editor was secretly watching
me from afar. They weren't, of course. But I had been spotted,
thirty-four miles away in Leeds, by Kenneth Young, then
editor of the *Yorkshire Post*.

The *Post*, which virtually smelled of roast beef, was a
grander, older established, more heraldic paper than the
Sheffield Telegraph. It had the aura of a stately home on whose
lawns intellectuals forever played cricket. Big businessmen
flapped it on the great-bellied old Yorkshire Pullman trains.
It was upmarket and 'county'. And, as a semi-national, with
a very jealous eye on the then *Manchester Guardian*, it was
quoted on TV on 'What the Papers Say'.

The *YP* had clout. And as its Woman's/Fashion/Cookery/
Gardening/House Beautiful editor – being Yorkshire, it
wanted everything for nowt – so had I.

I began to move, and even be courted as social editor,
in wider, grander circles. When our local lass – and my
contemporary – Katherine Worsley, married the Duke of
Kent, I had a prime pew-end seat in York Minster to describe
the union of York's slender White Rose with the White Horse
of Kent.

Geoff still wore out his passion and car tyres between
Sheffield and Leeds. Partly because of my fatal attraction,
mostly because my small, damp, but picturesque Yorkshire
stone cottage was almost on the boundary of Headingley
cricket ground.

I was settled in my Yorkshire roots, and sinking them deep,

when the *YP* decided to dress up its fashion pages by sending me to Paris for the French collections. That cut me back down to size. Provincial paper writers didn't even get seats at the big shows like Dior's. We scrimmaged at the back, or swung from the rock crystal chandeliers. Dior was always so packed, legend has it that one old fashion writer, who had a heart attack on seeing the new line, wasn't discovered until they swept her up with the smashed champagne bottles and broken gilt chairs.

It was here that I first saw Fleet Street's mighty, throned in their red plush chairs on the front row. Iris Ashley, the *Mail*, Jill Butterfield, the *Express*, Felicity Green, the *Mirror*. And they were pussycats compared with the terrifying old American tigers, like the *Sunday Times*'s Ernestine Carter, and the deadly *New York Times-Trib* duo, Eugenia Sheppard and Hebe Dorsey.

The Americans were awesome. *Vogue*'s editor, Diana Vreeland, and the Duchess of Windsor, who always sat side by side, had identical gleaming black patent skull-cap hair do's. Maybe they shared the same tin of polish. The grand old US gals had almost annual facelifts. In summer, while their scars were healing, they sat in a Mafia mob behind dark glasses. In winter, their frozen row of stony faces looked like Mount Rushmore. But even they weren't as fearsomely fascinating as a life-size porcelain doll from Italian *Vogue*, who never even glanced down at the notes she was making with a twenty-four-carat gold pencil. Rumour had it her face had been so often lifted that, if she bent her neck, her head would drop off.

Compared with expensive material like this, I felt like a remnant. And those scissor-tongued women needled me with their total dismissal of us provincial girls, or, worse still, their patronage. I knew I was as sharp, twice as cutting, and, given my chance, I could write them into the catwalk. It was Barbara Griggs, of the *Evening Standard*, who mentioned to me that the fashion editorship of a smallish but catchy fashion magazine, *Flair*, was up for grabs. On my way back through London I rang, and presented myself for the job. My experience was too narrow, my hips still too wide, but my self-salesmanship was massive, and they were pushed to fill the post.

When they wrote a week later to say I'd got it, it was too late to consider I detest fashion magazines, which I only glance at in the hairdresser's. *Flair* was in the Strand, within shouting distance of Fleet Street. From its roof I could see the *Daily Express*.

Back in Yorkshire, Geoff and I rifled through our lives to date, and came to a blank. He was pushing forty, and essentially a local paper man. The chances of him joining me in London looked about as bleak as sleeping on the Embankment.

'I won't go,' I wept, sacrificially.

'You're halfway there already, we'll just have to meet for weekends in Grantham,' said Geoff. 'I'm not going to spend the rest of my life being nagged that you could have been the greatest national journalist since sliced bread if you hadn't stayed in Yorkshire. Let's get going.'

He jumped up and started taking down the curtains. . . .

CHAPTER ✦ THREE

Living in the Shadow

I could hear the curtain hooks clattering along their runners. Someone was sitting on my bed, patting my hand and stroking my cheek. The chirpy little nurse who had checked me in.

'What happened?' I demanded. There were no politely vague 'Where am I?' preliminaries. Back from what seemed my split-second roller coaster trip into the dark, I knew exactly where I was. And why.

'You'll have to wait for Sister, pet, now just take it easy, Sister'll be here any minute.'

I was wildly awake and flaming mad with terror. 'I'm not waiting for anybody. Now what happened? I've a right to *know*.'

'I'm sorry, pet, I'm so sorry, but I can't tell you,' she said. She didn't have to now, of course. She'd just told me everything I'd prayed not to hear. She was a sweet kid, and I knew from her voice I'd wrecked her afternoon.

The curtains were swept clean aside, and I was swept into long, strong, bony arms. 'It was malignant,' the Sister said.

'I'm terribly sorry to have to tell you this, but you've got to
know and I thought you'd want it straight.'

'Is it out?' I pleaded.

'Yes.'

'Is it all out?'

'Yes, I was there, in the theatre.'

I didn't scream, swear, or even cry. Yet. When Nancy
Reagan was told she had breast cancer she felt 'as if I'd been
hit by a truck'. I felt as if I'd been shot.

I was looking at myself, from the outside, as if watching
one of those slow-motion gun frays. The Butch Cassidy bit
where the camera closes in on the already dead but still
standing victim, whose puzzled, glazing eyes seem to ask,
'What the hell did you do that for?' just before his twitching
body bites the dust.

I was falling through space, the little nurse's troubled face
fading into endless corridors of cream-painted ceiling. The
ritzy room wavering into focus was hushed with gentle voices,
and very plush. The fitted carpets were thick, the raw silk
drapes heavy, the eye-level TV now at the bottom of my bed
was the latest, largest, flat-screen model. Do people who've
been told, two minutes ago, that they have cancer, switch on
to *Neighbours*?

The lit-up console by my bed looked like the flight deck of
Concorde. Since I couldn't stand one mad moment alone with
my now shrieking, stampeding thoughts, I pushed all buttons.
Everything came on. The intercom, radio, TV, and a roomful
of swiftly running nurses. What could they get me? An ashtray.
Telephoning Geoff, my mother, Nicky, I chain-smoked twenty
cigarettes. It seemed academic, now, to worry about lung
cancer.

Our brief exchanges were dry and tearless. Arid of emotion
nobody dared express. We all seemed suspended in time, with
nothing to do, or say. Except Geoff, who had to let fifty people
know that the party was very definitely over.

'What shall I tell them?'

'The truth,' I said. I'd decided, the moment they told me
I'd got it, it was pointless trying to hide cancer in cosy excuses

like 'She's come down with 'flu.' 'But, if he rings, don't tell Gresby.' Our son was partying overnight with friends. Why ruin his Christmas before I might have to? Let him hang on, to the last minute, to all the fun, lights and music he could get.

'He'll ask for you,' Geoff pointed out.

'Tell him I'm at the London flat – no, don't, he might ring there. Tell him I'm out on a late job, but whatever you do, don't tell him what's happened. And don't come. It'll take you all night to ring everybody, and you know me in a crisis. Until I've come to terms with it, I've got to be alone.'

By now it was 5 p.m., and the editor's conference at the *Express* would have broken up. I rang Alan Frame, my closest colleague and personal friend, on the features desk.

'Well, how'd it go, how was it?' he asked in the eager voice I'd heard so many times, on so many crackling phones, through so many different time zones on assignments round the world.

'It was a shambles,' I said. 'It was malignant.'

In the short pause I could hear the distant chatter of friendly typewriters. 'Oh, *shit*!' Alan said slowly. He couldn't have written a more succinct headline for my day.

The surgeon arrived at 6 p.m. Even at the door he looked wary, as all medical people do when they're braced to be jumped on and shaken until their nerves rattle for reassurance they can't give. Totally panicked as I was, I realized 'How long have I got?' would sound like the lead-in to the commercials on *General Hospital*.

Grasping his held-out hands, I was morbidly fascinated that they had actually handled my ultimate terror. This man had seen The Thing. I wished I had. I needed to have faced the hidden enemy.

Weeks later, at Kent's Pembury cancer hospital, a nurse urged me, 'When you get depressed, thinking about cancer, draw it.' I didn't draw an octopus, perhaps because I couldn't face such a repellent predator, but sketched an oval potato with straggling roots.

'That's about it,' she said. 'Now think that the potato

has been dug up, but without the follow-up radiotherapy, fragments of the roots could still be in you. The radiotherapy may be hell, but it's scorching those roots black. Imagine them, better still draw them, shrinking shorter and shorter, and gradually rotting away.'

I was blatantly harassing the cornered surgeon. 'You're sure you got it all out?'

'I got out everything I could see,' he said. 'Until you've had bone and liver scans, we shan't know if, or how far, it might have spread.'

Spread! The word blazed through me with raging horror. I felt as if I'd just been splattered, at 90 mph, head-on into a concrete wall.

'What do you mean, *spread*? You said it was all out. I came to you as soon as I found the lump. I mean, thank God I got it so early.'

'No, not so early as you think. It was a sizeable lump,' he said, with enraging calm.

I wanted to knife him with his own scalpel. Why hadn't he let me decently die on the table, instead of dragging me back, maybe to lose the fight, breath by breath, to see my son grow up, with not even the palest, gauntest hope of seeing my grandchildren?

'You must control yourself. We can't know anything until we've done all the tests, and kicking and screaming isn't going to change anything,' he said. 'It may not have spread, and, even if it has, there's a lot that can be done.' How did he see my future, if any worth mentioning? 'You have a good chance of being fine.' And a fat chance I might not? 'Who can forecast these things?' he said. 'Who knows if we will live two years, or twenty?'

Spare me the updated *Rubaiyat of Omar Khayyam*, I thought savagely. As a son of Islam, you may have faith you've at least five hundred lives to come, but in my book, this isn't the rehearsal, this is all there is.

'I told you, my son is only sixteen.'

'You have told me several times,' he said patiently. 'Do you know why I wasn't here when you came round? I was doing the same operation on another woman. She's forty-one, with two children of six and three. I had to tell her it was malignant, too.'

I deserved the slapping cold flannel and the momentary cold shoulder. The tears of shame, rage and terror soaked the hands with which he'd done his utmost for my life. 'I know, I know,' he said gently. His face lightened. 'You're one of the strangest women I've ever met,' he said. 'I operated on you five hours ago, and there's one question you still haven't asked. The first question every woman asks as soon as she comes round.'

'What?' I said, listlessly dragging my mind back to the immediate present.

'How much do you think I took off?' he said.

In the choice between looks and life, I'd never even thought of it. Even now my hands didn't fly to what looked like my table-flat chest, strapped like Tutankhamun from collarbone to waist.

He looked almost disappointed. 'I didn't have to remove your breast,' he said. 'It was only a lumpectomy, not a mastectomy. You'll be able to wear low-cut dresses, even a swimsuit. When the scar fills out you won't even need to stuff tissue in your bra.'

At that moment, he might as well have been telling me he'd left two melons, instead of one, on the sideboard. Writing this now, I thank God, and Allah, which I know will make him smile, for his sensitivity, skill, and his cosmetically stylish, low-cut scar. I've always been proud of my bold front, and I'm thankful, now, that every centimetre of my womanhood he could save is still intact.

Even zonked with painkillers and sleeping pills, I dreaded sleep. My photographically trained mind always records the night before, and relives it, in a flash, the morning after. I knew that waking from pill-manufactured sleep would only be an ongoing nightmare, and that the bitterly cold light of dawn would crack me up.

In the suite next to mine, a middle eastern gentleman who'd suffered a mild heart tremor was wailing to Mecca like a full-blast minaret. Around midnight, he had a call to prayer for what sounded like all two hundred members of the Saudi royal family.

Private health care was beginning to rip apart my already threadbare nerves. It was fine for a nose job, if you can afford to pay through it, but I was becoming sick of the fake glamour of my soap operatic surroundings. Cancer is not a glamorous, satin negligee disease. And I'd enough stingy Yorkshire spirit left in my tattered breast to resent carving into a whole month's mortgage in a single lunch hour. I had to check out of this five star Heartbreak Hotel.

At 6 a.m. I rang Geoff and asked him to get me into our local Kent cottage hospital. Mid morning, my secretary, Nicky, arrived, looking as if her night had been a smudgey-eyed carbon copy of mine.

Somehow, we bundled my bandaged wreckage into my clothes, and made up my face. Normally a five-minute job, it took two of us half an hour, dropping everything all over, to shakily paint my now staring-eyed mask of utter despair. My life, such as it was now, felt shot through with Novocaine, pierced by screaming twinges of remembering I had cancer.

In the back of the office car, I screwed up the nerve to try an experiment I'd been putting off all night. Unhinged as it sounds, I'd postponed literally pinching myself. My dreams are rare, but when I have one, it's a Universal Studio production which seems to last for reeling, realistic hours. Please God, I physically nipped my still strong right arm, let this be a Technicolor nightmare in stereophonic sound. Nothing happened, except that I felt the pinch, and saw the hopeless, silly little flush on my forearm.

Checking into Edenbridge cottage hospital, I had to pass their lit-up Christmas crib. The scene hadn't changed since Gresby's adenoids, twelve years before. Baby Jesus's pink plastic arm was still raised in greeting. Lord, I snapped silently, you've certainly handed me one hell of a Christmas present.

But I felt strangely better in my narrow, clanking metal NHS bed, with briskly kind, no-nonsense nurses, too rushed off their swollen feet to cater to my every whining whim. Here, I felt obliged to shut up. For the first time in twenty-four hours, I wondered if I could learn to put up with cancer. Live with it, and even beyond it.

My GP's friendly face round the door killed off my short-lived courage. Over the fifteen years I'd very rarely seen him, we'd exchanged nothing but the odd bronchial cough and anaemic comment on the weather. Now he was my lifeline, and I was tangled in his stethoscope, breathing my last about my lost life, lost family, lost job, lost hair which was bound to drop out.

'That all sounds a bit drastic, don't you think you're rushing ahead a bit?' he said. Between dashing round to his surgery for hastily picked-up prescriptions for nothing really worth examining, I'd never before stopped to listen to his purring west country accent, cosy as a curled-up country cottage cat. 'We can't deal with anything until we know just what we've got.'

I knew what I'd got. 'Judging from the frozen section on what they removed yesterday, you had a grade two carcinoma,' he said. Where does that put me on the Richter scale? 'Grade one is small and very early, two is a fair-sized lump, three usually means a mastectomy, and four is spread throughout the breast and lymph glands, and perhaps even further through the body' – the way he ticked it off, like a shopping list, was actually quite calming.

'Let's take it that it was localized and is all out. With six weeks follow-up radiotherapy, that gives you a sixty per cent, or higher, chance of a complete cure.' And a forty per cent chance of missing next Christmas? 'No – a fair chance of a decent life span, though at some time, if you're unlucky, you might need further breast surgery. But why look for bad luck? You must know women still walking around ten, twenty, thirty years after even a radical mastectomy.'

The poor old beaten-up breast began to swell with some hope. 'Now let's take it at it's worst, and assume that it's spread,' the doctor said, gently but firmly pushing me up against an idea which, a few hours ago, would have driven me to total, freaked-out madness. 'That reduces your chances but there's still a lot that can be done, maybe over several good years. These days, it's not an automatic death sentence.'

He'd made his point. If Bob Champion could lose four stones, and his hair, without losing his head, and beat cancer to win the Grand National, why was I dropping out at the first fence?

Tentatively, my Christmas lights began to flicker back on. I thought of the back-breaking month's work Geoff and I had put into preparing for the party – three loaded Christmas trees, tinsel by the ton, a grotto of fairy lights, and the whole house blazing like Trafalgar Square. Should I have tried to go through with it?

It might have been just physically possible, the doctor said. But I'd have looked like Marley's ghost, and, by the time every woman had asked about my operation, and shown me hers, I'd have been climbing the Christmas tree without a ladder. 'They'd all have backed you into the bathroom for a private consultation,' he grinned. 'Mention cancer, and every woman has a tale to tell – most of it wrong.'

Two days later, back home, I was hit by what he meant. The now flower-filled house looked like a conservatory or the crematorium, depending on my mood. Along with the blood red streams of poinsettias, the phone calls began pouring in.

One of the first was from a chum built like Boadicea, with a voice like a brass gong, who doesn't need a telephone. She's only to stick her head out of her front door, half a mile away, and yell at her normal screaming pitch. 'My dear, I was S-H-A-T-T-E-R-E-D!' she shrieked, endangering even my rattling windows. 'Oh my God, you can't *imagine* the shock! I tell you, I was simply *shattered*!'

'So was I,' I chipped in, tartly, but it was lost on her.

'People who have cancer are so *brave*,' she boomed.

'I'm not – I'm scared stiff,' I was trying to say when she knifed across me with:

'Yes, you are, you're wonderfully brave. I've another friend with cancer who's so *brave* – she's fighting like mad but, of course, she's losing every inch of the way.'

How old was her expiring pal? Pushing eighty. 'But I've another friend of only forty-five,' she trumpeted. 'Since she had her breast off, she's travelled everywhere, and done everything. She's been marvellous – only now they've just told her it's spread to the other breast. Now, don't forget, if ever you need cheering up you know where I am,' she ended, slamming down her phone like my coffin lid.

I was braced for a phone call from Barbara Cartland, who had blanketed my bedroom with shocking pink carnations. The Queen of Natural Health and Beauty would not approve of radiotherapy, and what was I going to say when she commanded me to take two hundred daily vitamin pills instead? Actually, she was marvellous – a tonic in herself, flooding down the phone wire.

'Don't worry about a thing, darling. I've got this old chum who was dying of cancer years ago – I'd virtually picked out his wreath' (shocking pink enough, no doubt, to resurrect him). 'They fixed him back up so he's rushing around all over the place at nearly ninety, a fearful bore since he's absolutely ga-ga.'

The most memorable call was from a recent acquaintance in her late forties, an exquisitely turned-out creature, with an enviable figure, who used to be an Arden beauty consultant. 'I'd never have told you this, but now I think it might help,' she said. 'I had the same job done nine years ago.'

After twenty selfless minutes, uplifting me, her voice filled with tears. Had her cancer recurred? 'No, my daughter died of meningitis, two days ago,' she said, flatly. 'She was at Warwick University. She was twenty-one.' Her massive, unselfish kindness made me feel at once very small, and suddenly determined to try to be my age, and grow up, whether or not I'd be given time to grow old.

Back at the hospital, my husband arrived with an agitated bunch of flowers, and two Stephen King horrors I'd already read. Our in-depth, life-and-death conversation should have lasted far beyond visiting hours. It took us two minutes to discuss the cat and dog. After that, we stared at each other with a wild surmise, but neither of us said it.

Next morning, early, Geoff phoned me. 'I told Gresby on the way from the station where you are.'

'How did he take it?'

'Hard to tell.'

My son arrived, shades whiter than my sickbed sheets, with black circles under his eyes down to his sagging socks. 'My God, the idea of losing his mother must have half killed him,' I thought, panicking. I was ludicrously relieved when he told me he looked like death only because an underdone hamburger had backfired on him two nights ago.

He was giving off vibes, louder than a heavy metal concert, that he didn't want to hear the word 'cancer'. Since his ears were deliberately closed to it, I felt obliged, back at home, to shut my bedroom door, and my mouth, when he was within phone-shot of my conversations with friends.

Since Gresby and I are open books who can silently read each other, I hated and feared this deception. Surely the truth should come from me, and ought I to force him to face the issue? I reached the squirming point of saying, 'Look, you're no longer a child, I feel discourteous muttering secretively into phones. Is there anything you want to ask me?'

Very sharply, 'Mum, I'm not interested.'

'Gee, thanks,' I grinned weakly.

'I'm very interested in your welfare, I don't want to hear the gory details.'

If this is the future generation's faith in cancer cure progress, I'm a goner, I thought dolefully.

It was a male friend who gave me a much more sensitive and moving explanation of Gresby's uncharacteristically backing-off behaviour. 'He's worried about you, of course, but it's more complex than that. He's sixteen, right at the start of it all. He's got girlfriends. He *needs* to think of women's bodies as forever young and perfect. At his age, didn't we?'

Anyway, I told myself, he must know. If he can't add a removed lump to radiotherapy and translate carcinoma from the Greek, we're wasting £8,000 a year on Eton. I was cheered to feel my sense of humour regaining its health.

Once he was back at school, the inevitable happened quickly. Out of more than a thousand boys, Gresby was bound to drop on one whose mother had had cancer, and gone with the wind, virtually overnight. Studiously 'casual' phone calls about my health began coming thick, fast, and nightly. Since, like all schoolboys, Gresby is normally concerned only with the health of his finances, this really disturbed me.

At long last, after a hilarious night out seeing Maggie Smith in *Lettice and Lovage*, he came at me, dive-bombing from the blue, with 'Mum, did you have cancer?'

'You know I did.'

'Have you now?'

'No.'

'Could you live for ages?'

'I could, yes, but settle for twenty-five years, not thirty. I'm not a miracle like your Auntie Barbara Cartland. By the time I'm eighty-six, I'll be an infuriating old bat.'

That ended the subject, and the phone calls hectically dropped into Eton coin boxes. We were back to cheerful normality, reversing the charges to discuss pocket money.

Still in hospital, the night of our cancelled party, I had one more bitter pill to swallow. Our local carol singers arrived. Normally they come to our house and group themselves on our stairs, like a living oil painting, with their song sheets and lanterns. Hearing them shuffling in to the hospital ward, I crawled out of bed and shut them out of my room. I couldn't bear to see them, and prayed not to hear. Distantly, but bell-clear, *Away in a Manger* drifted like softly driven snowflakes under my hospital door. It was a cruel moment. And my starless night seemed long and hard.

My mother came down from Yorkshire, loaded with mince pies and love. As long as either of us lives after the cancer we've shared, like so much in our close relationship, I can never repay her for her care for me. To use a Yorkshireism she'd appreciate, she ran her blood to train oil for me. She pumped her strength into me, like a transfusion. She picked me off the floor of despair: 'Of course you can still write, you haven't had brain surgery.' She glued me back together: 'Stop wittering, Jean. If you're going to live the rest of your life scared stiff of dying, you might as well pack up now.'

Only once in all the weeks she hammered her own courage into me did we have a cross word. The fourth time in one day she said, 'I've been through it, I know just how you feel,' I snapped back at her, 'How the hell can you? When you got cancer your child was over fifty. Mine is still at school!'

Even as I said it, my eye caught a now sepia photograph of me, with my parents, taken when I was about three. A bouncing, healthy little beach ball in a too-tight swimsuit. I felt as if I'd knifed her in her own brave, damaged breast. 'I got that wrong, Mum, can you forgive me?'

'Forget it,' she said. It was the only tear I have seen her shed since I told her I had cancer.

Two days before Christmas, I presented myself at Kent's Pembury cancer hospital's radiotherapy department. If you've any small fame, you learn not to notice when people are staring at you. Or as a chum once gasped to me, 'God, have you any idea what it's like walking with you through Marks and Sparks?'

Normally, I've no idea. Like all so-called 'celebrities', and that's anyone who's appeared regularly on telly, I walk around inside a sort of second, thick skin, and don't feel the eyes boring into it.

But walking into radiotherapy, my skin was ripped away. Every glance wounded me. Every whispered 'Isn't that Jean Rook?' sliced through me, drawing blood.

Later, I was to be healed, not by sideward glances and behind-hand mutterings, but by much braver fellow cancer patients, marvelling outright, 'What on earth are you doing here?' to which I could cheerfully reply, 'Exactly the same as you.'

But now I was raw. And emotionally opened up, yet again, by the young cancer specialist who examined me. 'Do you think I'm going to die?' I begged him – I'd run out of clever ways of skirting round my mind's uppermost question.

'I know I'm here to cure you,' he said.

'And can you?'

'I think so. Fill in these forms for chest X-rays and blood tests, and I'll ring you tomorrow with the results.'

Tomorrow was Christmas Eve. On that of all days of the year, he surely wouldn't ring me if the news was bad? 'I shall ring you whatever it is, and whatever it is, you will face it,' he said.

I expected a brutal night. In fact, I slept like a Yule log, my terrors, blazing for so long now, probably burned out.

At 9.30 next morning, the phone rang. 'It's all right,' said the voice at the other end. 'It hasn't spread.'

'Can I live a good few years?'

'With luck, until you walk under a No. 19 bus.'

A Merry Christmas. Maybe even a Happy New Year. And, please God, bless us. Every one!

CHAPTER ✦ FOUR

Hitting the Street

*W*hen *Flair* magazine probed me on what I knew about colour photography, I'd blinded them with a spectrum of lies. 'Everything!' I beamed, radiantly. In fact what I knew about setting up a colour photograph would have fitted on the back of a picture postcard of Skegness, and still left room for what I knew about the fashion industry as well.

My *Yorkshire Post* pages had looked smart-ish, but were merely tacked together from second-hand, hand-out photos from the London and Paris fashion houses. The only creative 'fashion photographs' I'd been involved with were black and white, and more often greyish snaps, banged off by *YP* news cameramen, of local lasses in West Riding woollies, huddled on stone walls, surrounded by cropping sheep.

My humble room at the *YP* had been a cosy little eight foot by six foot paper-crammed pigpen. *Flair* was five doors from the mega-swish Savoy Hotel, and looked like part of it. I was stunned, my first morning, to find I now owned a fully-fitted eighteen foot by twenty foot office, four slick-hipped fashion assistants, two sleek secretaries, three slim-line ivory telephones, and a whacking great wardrobe into which I felt like moving – I was so Yorkshire-sick and crushed by the new-found power I hadn't a clue how to handle.

Much worse, I hadn't an inkling what my unwilling assistants were talking about. All four had applied for the fashion editorship, and loathed my guts which they intended to cut up into garters for being brought down from Wuthering Heights to boss them around. At my first hostile conference, I sensed they were braced to pick my seams, and, if they could find any threadbare patches, to slit my rapidly fraying confidence from top to bottom.

Well ahead of me, they had arranged to shoot the hat that would make autumn headlines on *Flair*'s front cover. When they innocently rolled out eight hats for me to choose from, and assumed I would be taking the photographic session to 'show them how it should be done', I knew they were hell bent on having my head. And handing it to *Flair*'s editor, Maureen Williamson, late of *Tatler* and *Queen*, in a be-ribboned hatbox.

Their unspoken insults, like a couple of the hats, were veiled. To add the possibility of physical injury, they'd arranged for the shooting on Tania Mallet, a model whose fearful temper was as ugly as her face, on every station bookstall, was beautiful.

I handed the Fearsome Four two hats apiece ('I will make up my mind when I've seen them on'), grandly paid the taxi fare to Hampstead, and, for what I prayed they didn't know was the first time in my essentially provincial life, stepped into a top photographic studio. And straight across a broad, pale pink paper path on the floor, leaving filthy footmarks. I didn't know that the background to a magazine cover was paper, suspended from the ceiling like an elephant's toilet roll. Or that I was supposed to take my shoes off.

I had put my foot right in it. Miss Mallet, tensed to tread on me, stamped hers. First fixing me with tigerish green eyes the size of emeralds, she examined the hats as if they were festering heads on poles. 'I think the whole lot are shit, and I wouldn't be seen dead wearing any of them,' she announced, obviously convinced she'd put the hatbox lid on my morning, so we might as well all go home.

My four thrilled assistants, purring round La Mallet's ankles, were watching me like lesser, but no less lethal cats. I took a short, very sharp breath. 'You're not paid by the hour to think, even if you're capable of it, Miss Mallet,' I said. 'All your head's good for is to fit inside the hats. You will try them on until I choose one. If not, you won't get your fee. Incidentally, I suppose everyone's told you you have a perfectly exquisite face?'

'Yes, they have,' she said, her gorgeous jaw dropping.

'Have they also told you you've got rotten legs?' I said, 'which is why I suppose all your magazine covers are head shots.'

If the photographer's Nikon had been a Magnum 45, Mallet, later to be a Bond girl in *Goldfinger* (the shots of her legs were distant) couldn't have looked more blown apart. Then she flung back her magnificent head, howling with laughter. 'That's the rudest thing anybody's ever said to me!' she snorted. 'I think that's just *great*!'

So did the now Friendly Four assistants, who'd put up with a lot from the much-feared Mallet, and never before seen her put down. In fact, Tania the Terrible and I later became good buddies. Although she was sexually straight as a hat-pin, it was Mallet who alerted me to a danger in my new profession which had never crossed my breezy moorland mind.

'For God's sake, don't *do* that!' she snapped one day when I automatically stretched out a hand to adjust the slipping front of a dress she was modelling.

'*Why?*' I leapt back from her cleavage.

'Because, you berk, a lot of the girls like it,' she grinned at my now fuschia face. 'The models who sell their stories to the Sundays may have laid male movie stars, but a hell of a lot of them prefer being all girls together in the dressing room, know what I mean? Don't look when a model takes her bra off – especially not sideways, in the mirror – and never touch. Unless you want to be lumbered as a raving dyke!' You live and learn quickly in the rag trade. From that day on, I've never even pinned up a hem on a live model.

Back at *Flair*'s office at the end, thank God, of my first day, I called another conference of the now slightly Frightened Four. Pointing out they were stuck with me, I suggested we hung together. From then on, bless them, they stuck to me like Velcro, and we became a formidable team.

Gradually I pieced together a working knowledge of fashion editing. Not that my ideas always worked. My greatest disaster was the Coat of Many Colours. When long-haired fake fur was the new sensation, that grand old Jewish Queen of the Sixties rag trade, Lily Mono, produced a stunning slim-cut coat, with a huge, turned-up fake fur collar. All in shocking pink. And I mean really shocking, the colour of Blackpool rock.

This was the shade Maureen Williamson turned when I informed her I was shooting the coat for *Flair*'s Christmas cover. 'Shocking pink will photograph purple, and I absolutely forbid it!' snapped Maureen, cheeks puce.

'It's the greatest coat this season, it'll make a killing cover, and I'm shooting it!' I fired back.

In the camera, the coat looked a peppermint pink sensation. I blocked my ears to the photographer's warning, 'You'll never get that colour true – it'll come up blueish on the transparencies.'

It came up royal purple. Pure pansy. Mighty mauve. But it looked astounding. There never was a magazine cover like it. The snag was there wasn't a coat like it, either. Mono's coat was unarguably pink. Mine was militantly purple. We had no time to re-shoot. When she found out, Maureen would strip me naked with her tongue, before she sacked me on one of the worst spots I've been in in my life.

Trembling like the fronds of her stupendous fake fur collar, I rang Lily Mono. 'Lil,' I said, 'the cover looks wonderful. It's a dream. The only nightmare is it's come out purple instead of pink. And *Flair* comes out next week!'

I thought Lil had died at the other end. 'I've got five hundred frigging pink coats here,' she choked eventually.

'How long would it take you to run up five hundred purple ones, and I'll sling in a caption, "it also comes in a shattering shade of pink"?' I said. 'Lil, it's that or my job!'

Sniffing vast profits, and nothing if not an old trouper, Lil turned her factory over to weekend overtime. Within days of *Flair* hitting the bookstalls, the coats, pink and purple, had sold out. The model resold in thousands. By February I was sick of the sight of women, like sticks of rock or Parma violets, in fake fur collars.

I was just as sick of *Flair*. Either you have a monthly magazine mind, or you haven't, and I was strictly a racey, pacey, daily newspaper journalist. *Flair*'s snail pace was killing me. If it had been any slower, we'd have been going backwards. Dedicated magazine fashion writers, of which I now knew I could never be one, can spin out a brief caption for hours. Then unpick it, and spend another day re-embroidering it. I could knock off *Flair*'s entire fashion wordage in a day. This left me thirty days a month to file my now long, glamorous nails, unchipped by a typewriter, and yawn through fashion shows. I had my hair done so often it began to drop out.

Flair belonged to the International Publishing Corporation, which owned the *Daily Mirror* in the days when 'Cap'n Bob' Maxwell wasn't as well known as the bloke on the Bird's Eye fish fingers packet. One Friday afternoon, IPC's great Welsh chief, Hugh Cudlipp, soon to be knighted, then lorded, called my office just as I was thanking God for the end of another tedious week. Could I see him? Now? Cudlipp was the sexiest man who ever made woman draw heavy breath. He'd a voice like a Welsh harp and looked like a cross between Richard Burton and Owen Glendower. Wicked rumour among IPC's female staff had it he was a sexual fiery dragon, and every woman who worked for him secretly burned to see his forked and swishing tail.

His summons was almost disappointingly strictly business. 'How would you like to be fashion editor of my new *Sun*?' he beamed.

'More than my life,' I replied, dazzled.

The still-under-wraps, not-yet published *Sun* had been the talk of Fleet Street, radio and TV for weeks. Its rising was to be a new, shining era in journalism. Nothing to do with Rupert Murdoch's eventual smash-hit, soaraway tabloid, IPC's *Sun* was to be a brilliant morning broadsheet which would singe the eyes out of worshipping readers. And any journalist who joined it would be an overnight star. It didn't happen that way, of course. The *Sun* rose, as in a fog, like a damp cinder, but more of that later.

'Miss X (he mentioned the name of the girl who foolishly turned down the job, which twenty-odd years later, it wouldn't be fair to repeat) has decided it will be too much like hard work,' Cudlipp said. 'The way she put it is that she doesn't want to be the only person with no time to turn up at her own dinner parties.'

Scrap dinner. Give me the *Sun*, and I'll live on fish and chips.

'Start on Monday,' said Cudlipp. God knows I was no smartly wrapped gift to the fashion magazine world, but that would leave Maureen Williamson only forty-eight hours to patch the huge hole I'd leave in *Flair*. By Monday, she couldn't even manage a bodged-up darn.

'Make it a week on Monday,' I hedged.

'Done,' said high and mighty Hugh, a man I've always loved, and often regretted, since I wasn't married at the time, that he didn't offer me the chance to prove it.

Maureen, a wrinkly Sloane Ranger true to type, always bolted for The Country on Friday lunchtime, and returned around noon on Monday. When I broke my news, she shot me a look darker than her inevitable Little Black Dress with its cluster brooch on the left shoulder, just like the Queen's. If the bother of replacing me hadn't wrecked her next three long weekends, I think Maureen would have been glad to see the still fairly broad Yorkshire back of me.

Maureen Williamson died of cancer three years later. To the end, she was still very grand, and stupendously brave. She wore a turban to hide her fallen-out hair. And a bright red, painted-on, old fashioned Duchess of Windor lipsticked smile to disguise her pain. I disliked her intensely. And admired her immensely.

Amy Landreth, the *Sun*'s Woman's Editor, was hell on high heels. My first female newspaper boss, and, I swear, my last. A former Cheltenham College Lady, with a schoolmarmish mind as neat as her desk, Amy was demanding, domineering, and, under her thumb, I felt like a squashed and wingless fly.

Since she herself had been fashion editor of the *Daily Herald*, which the *Sun* replaced, she was not only determined to control me. She even remotely controlled me, abroad, by rewriting my copy over the phone. I dreaded returning, flushed with red wine, to my Paris hotel bedroom, overflowing with her endless burbling streams of telexes and phone messages. Amy was mistress of the memo. She issued written orders, suggestions, random thoughts, ideas she'd had in the bath, like paperchains or ticker-tape.

I'd a slight counter-hold on her stranglehold on me. Amy was old *Herald* guard. What the *Sun* desperately needed was a transfusion of new blood, because its first appearance on the horizon had not gone to plan – certainly not the bold new plan eagerly worked on for pre-launch months.

On 15 September 1964 the *Sun* rose at dawn, in the biggest blaze of TV advertising in newspaper history. Even by 9 am the damned dull thing looked as if it was setting. Legend has it someone lost his nerve in the middle of the night, and all the new names and fresh features were ripped out. Next day what was published was a latter-day copy of the *Herald*, written by all its old, tried writers who'd been there since the day dot. And, by the swinging sixties, very trying most of them were.

Instead of a brave new *Sun*, miffed readers bought a nervous old *Herald*, packed with the dead paper's familiar, faded and flickering stars. Its only glow was its blood-red politics, and they were decades out of date. Its leaders read as if nothing but the paper's title had changed since the 1926 General Strike. The *Sun* hit the streets with four million curious readers, and sank to one million within a week.

Our slog was now to somehow climb back. To survive my tottering work load, I halved Amy's memos by hurling half of them into the bin. And so dropped my career's heftiest brick, which still weighs on me, twenty-four years later. One morning, under Amy's paper Everest, I found a picture of a teenager called Lesley Hornby, in an art college magazine for which she'd modelled. Across the schoolgirl's skinny knocked knees, Amy had blue-pencilled, 'Check this one out – she could be the great new find.'

I didn't bother. Deirdre McSharry, then fashion editor of the *Express*, did. Within twenty-four hours, the *Express* had renamed the unknown, six stones six pounds sixteen-year-old from Neasdon '*Twiggy*'! Within weeks, they'd made Twiggy's face her fortune, themselves a huge circulation grabber, and a total twerp of me. I felt like the Hollywood studio that turned down *Gone With The Wind*.

Amy Landreth didn't give me the sack. She didn't even gripe 'I told you so' about the historic lost scoop she herself would never have missed. I admired her as a gallant loser, thanks to my incompetence, and settled down to listen and learn with the respect I now realized she deserved. Amy, in her turn, scrapped the tonnage of crumpled paper, and agreed to brief me straight from her elegant, horsey mouth. Amy was no writer. In print, she read like a boring letter from your cousin. But she was a one-woman factory of brilliant ideas, and, when I began carrying them out, the *Sun*'s woman's page started making a name for itself. And for me.

One day she chucked me a photograph of Princess Margaret in a pair of diamond-patterned black stockings. 'Those are so damned old-fashioned she must have had them in her bottom drawer for at least two years!' she grinned. 'Why not say so in your own killer style?' We're talking about the days when royals were automatically, tediously 'radiant'. To print 'Where did Princess Maggie get those out-of-date Black Widow spider legs?' in 1965 was not only breaking new ground. It was smashing down the barbed-wire-topped barriers between Buck House and Fleet Street. My footnote on Margaret's 'fuddy duddy feet' made front page headlines. And *What the Papers Say*. Plus American, Canadian and Australian radio and TV, panting at all hours for interviews.

Mine was the first foot on the road to realistic writing about royalty, but I couldn't know what a wide path I was opening up. Or that, twenty years later, the tattier tabloids would be savaging the royals like bloodhounds, and slamming the boot into Prince Charles.

On the heels of all this Geoff and I married. Dogged as a Yorkshire sheepdog, he'd trailed me south, and landed himself a job with the Press Association. Geoff was an ace reporter, and his prestige was high. His dismally skinny pay packet was on the poverty line. We pooled our ideas, and cash, and decided to sink or swim together. My stingy proviso to becoming a wary bride – I felt safer single, living in sizzling sin – was No Children.

At thirty-one, I didn't like or understand children. I categorically didn't want one. No screaming, bilious little bundle was going to come between me and the top job in Fleet Street. 'So I don't think it's fair you should feel you've got to marry me,' I told Geoff.

'I haven't got to, but I'm going to – full point, end,' said Geoff.

My father, who never saw me as a day older than a forward fourteen, complained I was 'too young to know my own mind'. My mother was quite relieved to dust the shelf on which I'd been sitting long enough to form cobwebs.

My star on the *Sun* was still rising. In 1965 Ernestine Carter, dreaded doyenne of the *Sunday Times*, took a flyer on digging up Molyneux. Captain Edward Molyneux, an Englishman who pronounced it 'Mollie-nukes', was an ancient, but still just living legend. Back in the thirties, he had not only been the only British couturier to take on the French. He'd beaten them at their own fashion game and actually trained the great Pierre Balmain. He'd made yards of publicity by designing the old Duchess of Kent, now Princess Marina's, wedding dress. And stitched up his vast reputation by creating everything worn, on stage and off, by Noël Coward's glamorous leading lady, Gertrude Lawrence. Ernestine was not put off by the fact that the dear old boy now had only one eye, and had been wilting for fifteen years on the Provence carnation farm to which he'd retired in 1950.

'Thank God Molyneux is coming back!' Noël Coward warbled to *Women's Wear Daily*, bible of the US rag trade.

'One great name, *Molyneux*, says it all,' Mrs Carter lectured us at a flash London party to herald the reopening of his Paris salon.

The setting for Molyneux's come-back was sensational. His new salon was a line-for-line, dove-grey copy of his old thirties headquarters, on the same sacred spot – bang next door to Maxim's in the Rue Royale. The atmosphere at his re-launch was fraught. Nearly a thousand fashion writers were fighting to cram into the three hundred available seats, all terribly bitched off that Noël Coward, Gladys Cooper, and the Duchess of Windsor were wasting good space on the front row.

The clothes were terrible. Thirty years out of date. Boring, tightly tailored navy suits, with 'crisp little touches of white', and a few swathed evening dresses in which they could have shrouded the late Gertie Lawrence.

I rang Amy.

'How was it?'

'It stank,' I said. 'Any woman who's worn Mary Quant wouldn't be seen dead in any of it.'

There was a winded pause. 'Write it,' said Amy. My breath was short.

'Amy, the *Express* and *Mail* are twice as big as we are, and so scared of Ernestine they're bound to say it's a smash,' I said. 'And Ernestine will come out drooling on Sunday, if only to save her face.'

'Write it,' goaded Amy. At that moment of truth, I loved her.

I wrote it straight from the elbow. What I'm almost sorry now I didn't write, though Ernestine held it against me to her life's end, was the *Sun's* horrifying headline. 'F L O P Y N E U X!!!' was the streaming banner across our fashion page. The French pop newspaper, *Le Figaro*, went mad. Thrilled by England's second Waterloo, they splashed

'F L O P Y N E U X!!!' across their front page. The American fashion writers, all bosom buddies of American-born Ernestine, ripped off my epaulettes. But they printed my name, and the *Sun*'s.

As vile luck would have it, Ernestine and I were booked on the same flight back to England. She, of course, was in the snooty first class nose of the plane. My rear seat was nearly in the back lavatory. As we walked together from the airport lounge, me laden down with four jars of Dijon mustard in a plastic carrier, she with a bottle of *Vent Vert* suspended from her little finger by a gold string, Ernestine shot me a look that melted the tarmac. 'You were very, very naughty,' she breathed slowly and deeply. 'And very, very wrong!'

My demolition of Molyneux had no real strength to damage him. And certainly not after Ernestine's rave notices in the *Sunday Times*. Time, truth and the customers alone told. At Molyneux's next half-empty collection you couldn't have given away a press ticket with a crate of free perfume. His second house struggled on, even after his death, but the grand old man must have cursed himself for not sticking to farming carnations. Years later, I met a much older, frailer Ernestine at one of Ted Tinling's parties. 'You were very, very naughty,' she sighed. 'But you were right.'

'You were stuck with him, and I was just lucky,' I said. 'You're the one who'll go down in newspaper history as the great fashion expert. Compared with your work, I'm just one flashy headline.' I meant that. As a fashion writer, I wasn't worthy to hold Ernestine Carter's thimble. And about that, I *know* I'm right.

Once your name is worth selling, the trick in Fleet Street is to walk from one side of the pavement to the other for more money. When the dear little, now long-dead, *Daily Sketch* offered me twice my *Sun* salary, and its woman's editorship, I knew the glory would be brief, but, while it lasted, it would be banner by-lines and braying trumpets all the way.

The *Sketch* had been tipped, for years, to fold. Or, more thrillingly, to merge with its sister paper, the *Daily Mail*, to become the all-time Terrific Tabloid. Either way, I gave the

Sketch about two years to live, long enough to make a livelier name for myself.

The *Sketch*, under its editor, Howard French, was a little gem to work for. Not that Mr French's judgement (he wasn't the sort of chap you called Howard) was totally flawless. An ex-Royal Navy man, morally stiff as his moustached upper lip, he did not like 'nasty, titillating fashion pictures' in his paper. God knows why, but French was terribly titillated by armpits, which he banned. All my fashion models had to wear long sleeves, preferably demurely crossed over an unseen chest.

Mercifully, he liked legs. A lot. When the mini skirt was first hoisted, French went quite wild. We went inches further than the *Daily Mirror*'s pelmets: my girls wore virtually nothing below the belt. The day before he died, my beloved father, who thank God lived to see me on the success ladder, remarked to mother, 'If Jean's skirts get any shorter, they'll be collars.'

I loved Howard French, who retained his personal foibles up to his retirement. At the morning conference when the news editor announced, 'Jackie Kennedy is tipped to marry Aristotle Onassis,' we thought French would explode with a coronary.

'Jacqueline Kennedy was married to a President of the United States!' he informed us, as if we'd never known that. 'She cannot possibly be going to marry that greasy little Greek wop!' He never forgave Jackie-O, and gave the pictures editor a miserable time by trying to yank the Onassis engagement pictures off the front page, and bury them on page 26.

After French came English. A comparative kid in his thirties, and an absolute whizz, David English was the most demanding and inspiring editor I have ever worked for. A massive ideas man, everything he magically Midas-ed – and he touched every page of the paper – turned his staff's output to gold.

English exuded confidence in himself and his product. He never doubted his newspaper's influence, or his own strength. When the mini skirt dropped, he personally decided to winch it back up. The mini had evolved, hit its all-time high (nearly invisible) and fallen naturally back towards earth. But if David English pronounced 'what goes up, stays up', to hell with Isaac Newton.

For three months I ran his riotous 'Save Our Mini Skirt!' campaign. As a viable proposition, it hadn't a prayer, but, while more realistic publications' skirts went steadily down, our circulation raced up like our male readers' blood pressure. The streets might be empty of mini skirts, but at least we were still giving men what they wanted – crotch-high pelmets worn with kinky white boots.

English, we knew, was too big to be satisfied with the small *Sketch*. He had been brought in to merge the *Sketch* with its more powerful broadsheet stable-mate, the *Daily Mail*.

He announced I was to be the Total Tabloid's woman's editor the week I told him I was pregnant. I don't know which of us was more appalled by what we'd done. 'When's it due?' choked David, foreseeing me in anything but labour on the birth of his new paper. 'End of April.' The tabloid *Mail* was due in the first week of May. 'Great,' said David, sarkily, 'they can share a birthday cake.'

What had happened, I've always been able to assure my son, was no accident. My father's last, strangely Victorian moving words to me clung like his sweet memory. 'Get to the top, which you will,' he had said. 'But remember you've a life to live, and one day you'll grow old. Think what you have meant to me. Unless you have to, don't be a childless woman.'

At 38, I already owned a five-bedroomed pseudo-Tudor detached house in Petts Wood, Kent. Dear Pa had furnished it with some of his life-long antiques collection, and Mother pointed out, 'When I'm gone, you'll be lumbered with the rest. You're just like your father, you'll never throw an empty matchbox out, so you won't rest until you've a country mansion to cram it all in.'

She was spot on. My avaricious eyes were already straying to statelier houses and pastures new – at least ten acres. When Geoff and I were gone, there would be nobody for my hard-gotten gains but my already rolling Lincolnshire

Left: Rook at two — upwardly mobile.

Above: Which is the beach ball?

Below: Getting into the swing.

Mum and the forlorn barn owl.

My father, Horace Rook.

Those non-rose-coloured
specs.

At slightly sweeter
sixteen, I improve. My
father is standing behind
my grandmother,
Martha, and my mother,
Freda.

Left: The First Lady's first fur coat, which she no longer dares to wear.

Right: Getting on the ball — with George Best.

Below: Practice makes perfect — with Sacha Distel.

Looking for new
horizons.

Geoff in Cornwall.

Above: The apple of my eye nearly pokes it out.

Below: Traditional Christmas at South Riding with Great Dane Cressida.

Above: Laughter before the fall with Ted Heath.

Below: In on the making of Maggie — her first day in office.

relatives. I would slice them out of my will, or die working at it.

And I'd noticed a new, unpleasant trait in myself. I could no longer take children or leave them – so long as they were other people's. I'd go to any lengths to avoid them. The night I heard this strident voice in a hotel bedroom nagging, 'They'll have to move us, I can't stand that yapping kid next door,' and recognized this objectionable wingeing as my own, I looked deep into my narrowing, intolerant soul. If I was such a self-worshipping bitch, pushing forty, what sort of a fanged monster would I be at fifty, when it was too late?

'I think I made a mistake about children,' I riveted Geoff in bed one night. 'It was your bargain, not mine,' he said, but with vigour. Two months later I was pregnant.

Lord Rothermere, then Vere Harmsworth, owner of Associated Newspapers, was now in the agonizing throes of coupling the *Mail* and *Sketch*. And losing confidence in the 'star woman writer' of his great new paper at the same rate I was gaining poundage.

He rather reasonably suggested to David English that they ditch the *Sketch*'s ballooning Rook, and pick a preferably virgin woman's editor from one of the eight women writers on the broadsheet *Mail*'s existing 'Femail' staff.

'Trust her, she'll come up with the goods,' said blessed David. After such loyalty from English, I felt obliged to, even while the hours-old baby was chucking up his feed all over my copy.

Myth has it I refused to work with the old 'Femail' team, and personally sacked the lot, in one bloody night. *UK Press Gazette*, under the headline 'Night of the Long Knives', had me crashing dramatically through the barred door of Femail's office, swinging my axe like Clytaemnestra about to give her hubbie, Agamemnon, the blood bath. The *Gazette*'s opening sentence read '"My God, its all of us!" shrieked Femail fashion writer, Sandy Fawkes, as the *Daily Sketch*'s Jean Rook began knifing their jobs, one by one.'

In fact, I was still in maternity hospital when David English personally fired Femail, and it was only when I came back to a row of empty typewriters that I realized I was expected to do the jobs of eight women. At least until the new *Mail* finished paying for enough TV advertising to launch a space satellite.

My rapture at the tabloid *Mail*'s birth was miserably mixed with my sorrow for the *Sketch*. The little *Sketch* had been slaughtered to pump blood into its bigger, grander sister, and a newspaper which has laughed and cried with its faithful readers for sixty-two years dies hard. You don't switch it off with its silenced machines. A newspaper is a living creature, and its agonized, disbelieving last cries shudder through its empty building.

I was disturbed to find the *Mail* an unhappy ship, right from its spectacular launch. Perhaps because of the *Sketch/ Mail* merger – at the start, two people for every one job, and one bound to lose it – it was a back stabbing staff. And, given half a chance, your *Mail* colleagues would stab you front and sides for good measure.

The *Mail* whined, and griped, and could never raise a smile at its earnest self. My small *Sketch* column had now grown in status, was persistently quoted on air, and I was chuffed by a survey revealing that sixty-four per cent of my readers were men. But even under ever-inspirational English, I wasn't enjoying what should have been the Total Tabloid, but was in fact a greyish, moaning publication, with such vicious in-house politics that the walls ran blood.

On the eve of the *Mail*'s and my child's birth, I'd had a phone call at home from John Junor, not only editor of the *Sunday Express* since 1954, but, as its celebrated columnist, 'JJ', a household name and a huge journalistic force.

'Sorry about the *Sketch*,' bagpiped the great Scot, out of the air, since I'd never met him. 'What are you going to do?'

'Have a baby induced tomorrow morning,' I stunned him. 'But actually I've got the job with the new *Mail*.'

'I thought you would have, otherwise I'd offer you lunch,' Junor said. 'Anyway, if ever you feel like it, ring me.'

Now, after eighteen months with the morose *Mail*, I was ravenous for change. I rang Junor, not yet Sir John, who bought me lunch in Covent Garden. This in itself, I found out later, was a coup. 'JJ', a canny, not to say muck-mean Scot, didn't invent his fictional, dour little Highland village, Auchtermuchty, from nothing.

I suspected he condemned everything on the modest menu as auchtermuchty, but I was too engrossed meeting 'JJ' (editors are rife, fine columnists are rare) to fuss much with food. The meal wasn't helped down by terribly talkative Reggie Maudling, God rest him, then Home Secretary, who burbled over and asked if he could join us. Reggie seemed to have set himself the challenge of winkling a free lunch out of Auchtermuchty. He had about as much chance of becoming Prime Minister.

I'd heard, but not believed, that the *Sunday Express*'s big chief never took a wasteful taxi if a cheap wee bus was passing. Sure enough, Junor knew of 'five handy buses' that stopped outside the *Express* building.

Parting outside the black glass Lubianka, he suddenly said, 'Why don't you write to the *Daily Express*?' 'Why doesn't the *Daily Express* write to me?' I smiled, as near demurely as I can get.

That afternoon a note shot across Fleet Street from *Express* editor, Ian McColl. 'I admire your work. Why don't you join us?'

Conducting a liaison with an alien editor is as tricky as having an illicit love affair. Trickier because, with editors, you can't do it in the dark. You meet in unpopular places – never the Savoy Grill, which is wall-to-wall editors by 2 p.m. And you pray there's no ear-wigging fellow journalist at a nearby table, drinking it all in with his Châteauneuf-du-Pape.

A shrewd but open-faced little Scot, McColl laid his cards, and marked mine, on a downstairs, dim-lit corner table at the Waldorf. He would pay me a staggering amount more than the *Mail*. I would have a free hand. I suspected, rightly, he meant an empty hand – the *Express* proved as mean as the *Mail* with back-up staff. I liked his approach, and him, gave my word, and prepared, a month later, to sign a contract.

To report that David English was displeased is the grossest understatement I've ever typed. He turned the air blue and put a match to it. He made a counter offer that the Godfather couldn't have refused – massive money, a seat on the Board of Associated, a trust fund for the baby, and paid holidays in perpetuity. I'm bound to add it's not that I'm so valuable. Nobody is. I just happened to be the current symbol of the bloody running battle between the *Mail* and the *Express*.

English even sent Fleet Street's legendary lay-out genius, Harold Keeble, down to Kent at 2 a.m. with a counter contract. Keeble, who'd never expected to see me without make-up, in a bathrobe, had a shocking night.

So did I when I realized I must make a choice that would have dismembered the baby in the King Solomon case. I'd never see another offer like Associated's, but I had led the *Express* up the primrose path, and to slam the door in its face now would make my name stink in Fleet Street's gutters like rotten cabbage. And at the bottom of my greedy little Yorkshire heart, I knew the *Express*'s bigger, louder platform meant more to me than the *Mail*'s money.

My parting with the *Mail* was misery. In the end, which I suspected would be nasty – David English was going to have his way in that at least – I cleared my desk at 6 a.m., and bolted to Kent, leaving the legal eagles to fight it out. English threatened to hold me to my two-year contract, even while he handed my column to *Mail* feature writer, Lynda Lee-Potter. In this case, by the time I left the *Mail* building, my forgotten name would be so dead that the *Express* would be buying an expensive corpse.

David English, now knighted, never knew what it cost me, and not in cash, to split with him personally. Even after seventeen years, and only two accidental, and very chilly meetings, I still regard him as the editor's editor.

I regretted leaving Vere Harmsworth, Associated's big, deceptively bumbling, but upright proprietor. I still treasure, in untouched black tissue, the Harrods layette he sent for my new-born baby. The baby couldn't wear it. Little Lord Fauntleroy couldn't have worn it. It was all blue angora and satin on which it would have been sacrilege to burp.

The future Lord Rothermere's parting shot was 'One day

you will work for me again'. That day is passed. The long-rumoured *Mail/Express* merger got stuck at first base. I suspect rheumatism will get me, and Rothermere, before we get back together.

But Sir David English doesn't forgive, or forget. Since my name became worth looking at, *Private Eye* has always peered, squinting viciously, into my private life. I never minded the *Eye*'s caricature of me as the scurrilous hackette, Glenda Slag, mainly because I didn't regularly read it. I daren't. It was too near the mark. If any more of wittily written Glenda had rubbed off on me, I'd have ended up as her carbon copy, instead of the other way round.

But my bayed-after blood was supposed to run colder when David English set the *Mail*'s gossip-columnist, Nigel Dempster, and his team of snarling terriers on me. For weeks the *Eye* hacked me into pieces. When Jocelyn Stevens, unaffectionately dubbed 'Piranha Teeth', took over the *Express* management, only months after I'd joined, the *Eye* bulged with gleeful vitriol.

One night, two minutes before I was to appear, live, on Clive James's TV show, a cameraman handed me the *Eye*'s latest view that: 'Piranha Teeth can't stand the vapid ramblings of Rook. Rumour has it he would pay the clumsy Dodo bird her three-year contract, and £25,000 on top, if she'd only fly away.' I was elated, and the James show was a smash. For that money, I would fly into the mouth of hell.

In fact, 'Joss the Boss', as I knew Stevens, became a great personal friend. Perversely, so did Nigel Dempster, over the years he savaged me. You'd have to be dead not to like the urbane Nigel, even while he's carving you up.

So now I stood on the Art Deco doorstep of the mighty, mystical *Express*. Ever since Beaverbrook, wild, colourful rumours about the *Express* have run rife through other envious papers. Like, 'The expenses are so fantastic, a reporter once hired a helicopter from The Savoy back to his office.' And, less cheering, 'If they don't like you, they literally kick you into the gutter outside El Vino's.'

Overnight, I was Fleet Street's First Lady. Over seventeen

years, I was to survive eight editors. And be roasted by the seventh, Sir Larry Lamb, who hated my guts almost as much as I'd have been overjoyed to grill his. I was to interview Margaret Thatcher nine times. Fly round and round the world like a gilded moth. And be the first journalist to walk into a cage with a pair of man-eating Bengal tigers.

So why was I such a cowardly lioness that I dreaded being caged, alone in an empty room, with a radiotherapy machine?

CHAPTER ✦ FIVE

The Infernal Machine

*W*alking along the corridor to a warning sign outside the
radiotherapy department, 'NO ADMISSION BE-
YOND THIS POINT', had been the worst. A trip to an
unknown scaffold. 'Everyone feels like that the first time,' I
was assured by the girl who led me through the barrier. 'Once
you've met the machine and had your first treatment you'll
be much less agitated.'

Now I lay on a plank-hard couch with one arm above my
head. The radiotherapist and two radiographers surveyed the
swelling scene. In a mirror opposite, so did I.

Since teenage, I'd been proud of my size 36C, perky first
prize melons. Now I wished I had third prize tomatoes, or
even a couple of grapes. There would be so much less for their
infernal machine, lined up on my left breast, to get at.

I hadn't liked showing Geoff my mangled assets. We were
long past Romeo and Juliet, and getting hoary for Antony and
Cleopatra, but calling him into the bathroom to view my
damage was a far, sad cry from my blue-satin-nightgowned
wedding night.

'Marvellous!' said Geoff, putting on his glasses for a closer look. 'Amazing what they can do these days, you can hardly tell!' It was a naked lie, though it looked convincing enough with a bra on.

Now, even bare, my excavated hillock struck me as a fair mound to be exposed to what I'd been told was terrible treatment. I knew all about radium, of course, from school science. I knew that Marie Curie, who discovered it, fell to bits at sixty-seven, and that you can find her still horribly active grave in Sceaux, in northern France, with a geiger counter. Even her notes are alarm-locked in a lead-lined drawer in Paris, and can't safely be opened for 1,600 years without frying whoever touches them.

When I relayed these gems of knowledge to my examiners, the radiotherapist (a medical expert on radiation) and the radiographers (experts trained to give the treatment) realized they had a sizeable job on their hands. Besides my body, they'd have to sort out my mind if they were to help me help others by eventually writing sensibly on something about which I obviously knew nothing but old wives' tales of terror.

'Fighting off wild rumours about radiotherapy is the hardest part of the work,' they told me. 'We've had patients who actually ask how many hours they'll be locked up, and is it true we leave them under the machine until the pain is so unbearable they crackle and give off sparks.'

Forget radium, they told me. It is not radium they use, but cobalt which, breaking down, releases gamma rays which destroy any left-over malignant cells. 'You won't feel a thing during treatment,' they soothed me.

When they added, pressed, that the beam from their magnificent machine could zap through solid steel or a concrete wall like a buttered needle, I nagged to know what it did to my non-malignant cells.

'Normal cells repair themselves four times faster than cancer cells,' they cheered me, 'but you may have some skin reaction.' Just how my skin reacted, I'll shelve for later, or you may not want to go on with this.

I was told, to my horror, that I wouldn't be able to wash my left side, from the waist up, for the entire six-week course.

Surely by that time my best friends wouldn't even want to leave flowers on my doorstep, let alone visit? 'Radiation knocks out your sweat glands, you'll have no trouble there,' they assured me. 'And you'll have no problem with hair under your arm – it drops out.'

I hadn't realized the palaver you go through before treatment even starts. They don't just point their machine at you and hope to hit the bullseye. Lining up a patient for the gamma rays is like those *Day of the Jackal*-type films, where the assassin spends hours in the empty rented flat opposite, pin-pointing his hair-trigger target. They measure you up with plastic rulers and spirit levels, then mark you out, like an architect's blueprint, with coloured felt-tip pens. 'What if they rub off?' I worried about the drawn-on arrows which made me look like James Cagney in a thirties convict movie.

'If they start fading over the weekend, your husband can re-do them with a felt-tip,' beamed the radiographers. Oh, great! My husband gets nervous zipping up the back of a dress.

Some patients feel claustrophobic about the fifteen foot by ten foot windowless room in which they're left alone with the machine. At Pembury, a wall-wide mural of Canadian pines, reflected in cool blue lakes, is supposed to help. For the first month of treatment, it does. The last ten days you dream of leaping off your couch, and plunging your sizzling boob into the mural.

I wasn't troubled by the bunker-like room, or by being left alone – though I was shaken by the speed with which the radiographers bolted just before a siren sounded, and a flashing red light above the sealed door warned that the machine was ON. If it's all so safe, why do they rush for shelter as from a nuclear attack? 'You only get five minutes a day – two and a half hours in all in six weeks. We're in it for life,' they calmed me by explaining.

The machine bleeps 230 times, for two and a half minutes, on each side of the breast. You feel nothing. This is what I was beginning to hate about breast cancer. You feel nothing before you discover it. And nothing again while you're being pumped with cell-killing rays. Cancer is such a nothing *something* inside, and it's this that appalls.

The greatest discomfort in therapy is when they cram your breast into a plastic case as if it were some Cartier diamond, and pack heavy little plastic 'sandbags' inside the casing to hold you steady. Your every breath is monitored, by microphones, by the watchers through the ray-proof viewing window, and two closed circuit televisions are focussed on you, one on your face. This hurts. There's nowhere to hide your grief, or your fears.

'You can breathe normally, but it's important that you lie quite still,' I was commanded by the *Patient's Guide to Radiotherapy – Your Questions Answered* booklet with which I was issued. The first time I began hectically wriggling the itching nose I daren't scratch, a voice through the mike cracked me up with 'Doesn't that always happen when you're up to your elbows in flour in a pastry bowl?'

The bond between the patient and, in my case, two young women radiographers, becomes very strong, and precious. At first, cancer cases want to talk about nothing but The Thing. How they found The Thing. How they fear The Thing. And what can the radiographers do about it? And are they sure? And will it work?

Gradually, later, you begin to take an interest in the off-duty lives of these kindly, splendid people who are dedicated to saving your life. One of my young attendants was surviving the trauma of moving house. The other had a schoolboy son, and a lovely amateur contralto voice, and sang locally in the evenings.

I was heartened by their relaxed normality. Surely they'd be paranoid if they were daily dealing with death? 'The cancer you read about is always the famous person who's died of it, and of course there are cases we can't save,' the girls told me one lunch hour, as we gossiped on my couch, swinging our legs. 'But if our job was all depression, who'd want it?

'The cases you never read about are the ones who come back ten, twenty years later. One of the happiest things about

66

the work is to be in town, shopping, and waved at from across a street by a patient who came to you, looking absolutely terrible, five years ago.'

Little things about the treatment irritate. Every part of your body, of course, the split second they sound the siren for complete stillness. And the fact that, for the whole six winter weeks, I could wear only non-frictional pure cotton. At the end of a month, my two nightly-washed cotton bras were dishrags, and I'd never expected that a Caribbean cotton T-shirt, now advertising 'Surf Antigua' across my damaged chest, would come in for such a ghoulish purpose. For bitterly cold days, Gresby gave me an outgrown cotton sweatshirt. The hospital fell about at the logo across my battered bosom: 'Dire Straits'.

After a month, I was beginning to take as much hammer as my ragged undies. I was terribly, permanently tired, and depressed, over and above having cancer. Some days I felt swamped, overwhelmed by misery. At my lowest, I would rush into the windowless room, and gush with tears. 'I'm not scared,' I bawled, fairly truthfully. 'I'm just so bloody sick of not being myself. It's the *Daily Express* Boat Show this week, and I know it's stupid, but I'm crying remembering all the thrilling stunts I wrote up in other years. I was once winched one-hundred-and-twenty feet into a rescue helicopter in the roof.'

The head radiographer patted me, sweetly. 'You're crying for everyday life, for before cancer life – everyone does. But you'll learn to live again once this is over,' he said.

At first, I had almost loved the machine. It looked like a cross between an old-fashioned diver's helmet and the back end of a concrete mixer, with a greenish-yellow eye which opened to shoot out its cancer-blasting rays. When it swooped on me, on its long metal neck, I saw it as a life-saving friend. The fact that it had done twenty-four years' service, and was missing flakes of faded NHS paint, gave it a faintly chummy aspect.

But the final week, I detested it. They had casually mentioned 'some possible skin reaction'. They hadn't hinted at

just this side of being flayed alive. Thankfully, my gynaecologist had, before he left for post-Christmas holidays in South
Africa.

'I'm going to take a flyer and tell you what nobody else
will,' he phoned. God, I'm going to die! 'You're going to pick
out your outfit for Gresby's wedding if you do as you're told
and think about the thousands of women walking around
who've been cured,' he snapped.

'I've only called because you won't be able to get me, and
towards the end of the treatment you'll need reassuring if I
know you. Remember how you swore blind you wouldn't
suffer post-natal depression? And how shattered you were
when you grizzled all through the fourth day after the baby
was born, just like any other woman?

'What you've got to know is that radiotherapy is an increasing depressant. You'll feel very low towards the end, and since
you've a big breast with still very smooth skin for your age
you may burn quite badly. The way you whittle, that's when
you'll decide it's all going wrong, and you're wasting what
little time you've got left on useless treatment. I'm telling you
now, it *won't* be going wrong, and you're *not* wasting your
time. So if you reach the point when you think it is, remember
this phone call, and hold yourself together.'

I'd reached that point. Those final days, like the rough,
burned skin on my breast, were dark. The radiotherapist
advised me, 'Write it all down now if you're going to write
about it at all, because, once it's over, it'll be like the pains of
childbirth. You won't remember it.'

I didn't tell him I've total recall of every pant and shriek
of the ten hours' labour before my Caesarian. Perhaps it would
be as well to get radiotherapy down on tape while it was
red-hot.

On the tape of my final four days of treatment, a weary
voice I hardly recognize as mine records ... 'This is what
Dante's *Inferno* must have felt like. This must be hell on earth.
The heat comes from inside me, like some grim super-sunburn.
I generate my own heat, so scorching I can feel it on my cheek
if I bend my head. It's as if someone were putting a cigarette

lighter to me – I feel the flames jump the gap across my breastbone, and into the other breast.

'It feels like flinging yourself out on the beach in ninety degrees of Greek sunshine the first day of your holiday, and then spending the fortnight in bed. Only I can't hide under the cool sheets. I have to go back every morning into the sun. Red raw, and burned to death, I've still got to go out into that bloody, relentless sun. . . .'

Listening to it now, this is shaming stuff. I was coping only with the aftermath of one removed rotten walnut. One very old lady who often sat next to me in the queue of tatty candlewick NHS dressing gowns, waiting for our turn, had a growth on the side of her tongue. Barely able to swallow, and nearly speechless, she still croaked jokes about everything tasting the same – of nothing.

A stricken yuppie, who'd lost all his hair, and part of his head, drove his wheelchair as stylishly as a BMW down the peeling hospital corridor, hung with framed Constables from Woolworths. Asked 'How are you today?' he was always 'Fine!' When he kindly asked you back, you felt obliged to tell him you felt great, too.

With three treatments to go, my skin agonizingly broke. Since you can use no soothing metal-based ointments which argue with cobalt, you tear apart like crumpled crimson tissue paper. My only brief relief was a daily dosage of old-fashioned Gentian Violet, a lotion I hadn't seen since my battered and bruised hockey-hood. Gentian Violet is all it sounds. A yellingly violent purple, and hideously indelible on everything it touches. Bang went the last of my T-shirts and two new duvet covers.

I had decided, the moment they told me I had cancer, that I wouldn't put finger to typewriter during my illness. I would hide out, cave in, leave the *Express* totally, for three months, to come to terms with my traumatized life. But Christmas was barely over, and my treatment hardly begun, when my blessed mother slipped in her cutting 'Why can't you write – you haven't had brain surgery?' She was right, dammit. Wednesday's page 9 of the *Express* was mine, my property for sixteen years. The paper couldn't leave a three-month hole. They would have to fill my space with another writer.

And, after three months, what if I forgot how to ride the bicycle, while my stand-in stamped and screamed that she wouldn't give me my bike back? Of all that I'd lost – a piece of myself, peace of mind – I was damned if I'd lose my *Express* column. I rang Nicky, my faithful touchstone. Could I do it? 'Why not, you're the same person, aren't you?' she said.

I hadn't the confidence, or, I suspected, strength, to give birth to my page, in intensive labour, the day before it appeared. I daren't leave it, as I always had, until 5 a.m. on Tuesday. On the Monday night, I doodled, ridiculously nervous, with a couple of pieces. They read all right. There seemed to be no lumps missing in my talent to aggravate and amuse.

Next morning, I whipped up the courage to ask Pembury if they could put my 2 p.m. appointment back to 4.30, and could I have a shot at the column? 'So long as you rest physically, it might focus your mind and take it off the treatment,' said a mercifully regular Rook-reading radiographer. Now I screwed up the nerve to commit myself to the paper. 'Keep my page open tomorrow,' I phoned them. 'I'll fill it.'

Admiring my name in print, next morning, gave me more pleasure than I'd had in thirty-one years in the business. It was a tangible resurrection of my life as I'd known it BC (before cancer). I was still the person I knew, Jean Rook of the *Daily Express*.

I missed one column – the week the treatment finished, which was just how I felt, when the district nurse had to come twice a day to dress my spectacular wounds. I looked like my own flaming sunset. Just as everything broke down, and I couldn't bear even a sheet on me, Gresby rang to ask if he could bring a girlfriend for the weekend. No. Yes. Must. Life had to go on. Especially his life, at sixteen.

I stayed in bed to hide the physical mess, and the fact that I looked ghastly on my feet. The youngsters visited my bedroom, and perched there, as uncomfortably as healthy people do among the alien Get Well flowers. They made me laugh. When they'd gone, I cried. They were so fresh, unmaimed. They had it all to come. They were tomorrow. And yet they were my yesterday, because it seemed like only yesterday that I was sixteen, and light, happy years away from unimaginable cancer. And what of my now shortened, darkened tomorrow?

I was becoming a dragging nag to myself, and everybody else. Shrewdly, Geoff and my mother restored my sense of humour by refusing to humour me. When I flung myself, eyes and hair streaming, at Geoff, because my hair drier wouldn't work after the agonizing hour it had cost me to wash my dead straight locks, wrecked by radiotherapy, he sternly demanded who put the plug on it. A Fleet Street chemist. 'Well, it's not on properly, and damned dangerous,' said Geoff. 'I could be dying, so who cares?' I crackled dramatically.

'You could have been electrocuted, and then where would your cancer be with nothing to go at, and you with nothing to talk about?' he cooled me down with a blast of cold reason.

One morose morning, the tenth time I snapped and growled at him to take the dog out, and then collapsed, yapping and snarling against his chest with, 'Do you think I'm going to die?' he grinned, 'I wish you bloody would.' We were struggling back to normal.

Gradually, the crematory heat and the self-triggering burning bullets in my breast subsided. I stopped peeling. I only yipped with pain when I automatically turned over to my life-long sleeping position – flat on my face, crushing my left boob like a poached egg.

Two weeks later, the radiotherapist examined my cooling, but still shocking pink breast as if it were something hung in the Royal Academy. 'Lovely!' he enthused. 'That's really lovely!' I preened myself like the front line of the Folies Bergère.

What now? 'You come back in two months,' he said. 'Then three, then six for a while, then a year. I'm thirty-five, so over the next twenty years we'll be seeing a lot of each other. But you must enjoy life between check-ups. Sweat like hell the night before you come to see me – everyone does – but, for the rest of the time, forget it. Learn to live in the shadow, and enjoy the sun more.'

LEARN TO LIVE IN THE SHADOW AND ENJOY THE SUN MORE. This phrase is now printed, in headlines, on my heart. But before I could learn to live in and with my shadow, I had to pass through the haunting shadow of the death of my dear friend, Diana Dors.

CHAPTER ✦ SIX

Diana's Final Reel

*D*iana Dors' final letter to me, on aquamarine, gold-headed notepaper, is framed in my study under the *Express*'s last photograph of her. She's draped on a leopard-skin couch by her indoor swimming pool, flanked by a pair of ebony panthers. And poured into a skin-tight, sex-soaked black dress, with cleavage into which whole armies of men could plunge. She writes. . . .

My dear Jean,

I thought I'd just drop you a little note to let you know how things are progressing. At the moment, I'm imprisoned in Pinewood Studios, filming *Steaming* with Vanessa Redgrave and Sarah Miles – come down for lunch if you have time.

Everything is going amazingly well for me this year. Health is fine, according to the doctors. The Variety Club is giving me a tribute luncheon in the autumn. My diet progresses – I've lost even more than on TV-am in October, and am hovering round the old fifties weight mark, so it *can* be done. Immediately after the film I'm off to America for several television shows.

Oh yes, and here's the best news of all. At Christmas, I've been asked to appear as Fairy Godmother in a pantomime in the West End!

Well, it's just spring, and it looks as if this is going to be the summer of my life with a vengeance!

Love,

Diana.

The letter is dated 25 February 1984. Nine weeks later, on 4 May, Diana died of cancer, aged fifty-two.

Her last message to me, phoned from the hospital, ten minutes after her death, by her husband, Alan Lake, was 'Let Rookie know first, and tell her I'm sorry I couldn't give her an exclusive on this one, but the ending wasn't the way it was rehearsed.'

Only Diana could have managed this marvellous, B movie exit line, even on her deathbed. As only she could have noticed, just before The End, that her famous necklace, its gold letters spelling out DORS, was upside down. It had been taken off, for the first time in decades, for her final operation, and put back on by a nurse when she realized Diana's time was running out. At Diana's last-breath request Alan Lake adjusted it, moments before she died in his arms. In true Golden Oldie style, Britain's only blonde bombshell was buried in that necklace and her most sensational gold lamé evening gown, with a flowing matching cape. Her trademark platinum hair was combed out long and straight.

The sex queen who stopped a Cannes Film Festival by teetering down the prom in a mink bikini once told me, 'I did have a fabulous figure – 37-22-35, better than Monroe's. But the face was never much – little piggy eyes and rubber tyre lips, which is why I wear all the candy floss hair to hide it. I haven't seen my hair's real colour for thirty years, and I don't want to. If they stick my head on a pole, it'll always be blonde.'

For two years I'd watched Diana fight the cancer which was destroying her once fabled hourglass body. And seen her lose, day by day, inch by inch. Because I'd given her my word – 'I know you only cover big stuff like royal funerals, Rookie, but promise you'll write mine' – I was in there, to the last, with my notebook.

Typically, Diana had planned her own final reel. She left her last word that there must be no barricades round the tiny Sunningdale church which would have fitted into the kitchen of her nearby Berkshire movie mansion. That the service should be relayed to the public outside, still trying to press close to her. And that, at the climax of her mass, the church's glass doors should be thrown open to let in her ordinary, faithful fans. They had prayed so fervently for her recovery, they had every right to file past her pale gold coffin. In the shivering May sunshine, headscarfed everyday folk, with children and plastic shopping bags, mingled with the minks and Mercedes of showbusiness's glitterazzi.

Little Diana Fluck, from Swindon, the 'ugly kid who knew I was one day going to be blonde, and a film star, so I worked hard for Diana Dors, I spent thirty years creating her', was always grateful for the publicity she loved. Her funeral was the last thing she could give her worshipping public, and the last thanks she could offer to the press who admired and liked her. To the last, and beyond, she was the ever-open Dors.

When he told me of her death, Alan Lake had wept, 'Whatever shall I do now? I can't live without her!' That May day, he was demented, hunched, his eyes scarlet-rimmed as the single rose he threw, howling like a lost animal, into her grave. I was ashamed to be relieved to get away from this wild, wasteful grief which he couldn't control, even for the sake of their fifteen-year-old son, Jason. Diana, dammit, would have battled on for her teenage boy.

Cramped in the Datchet phone booth from which I telephoned her funeral to the *Express*, I remembered the little boxes in which she and I used to sit for ATV's crossword quiz, *Celebrity Squares*. 'If I get much fatter they won't be able to cram me into my box,' she used to joke, balancing her bulk on tottering spike heels. 'It's ironic that, when I looked like an hourglass, I never thought about time. You don't put weight on, do you? Four stones just creeps over you when you're not looking. Suddenly you look in the mirror and see this marvellous old Hogarthian whore.'

I'd said my God-speeds to my old mate under the pink-blossomed apple tree Alan had planted at her feet. Since I don't need stone-made memories, I didn't expect to go back there. Five months later, under the tree now covered with bitter little crab apples, I was watching Alan Lake buried in the spot where he had spent hours, crying and calling to the lost wife on whose wreath he had written 'To my own sweet love – only a whisper away.'

Half an hour before Lake shot himself, in Jason's bedroom, I was probably the last person on earth to speak to him. I'd read in the paper, without surprise, that Diana's beloved movie mansion was to be sold. I knew she had died virtually broke. And had flogged herself towards her death by taking on any work she could get, even when her cancer was advanced, to keep the only wolf that had never whistled at her from the door.

'You can tell 'em the "ebony" panthers are really only concrete glass fibre,' said the brave woman who never concealed anything but the lighting above her circular bed. 'But don't tell 'em the "leopard skin" couch is crimplene, the "white fur" carpet's fake, the old white Rolls is a rust bucket, and the "snakeskin" wallpaper's peeling.' I didn't tell 'em. I've told no-one, until now that it no longer matters, that the tiled sunken bath was chipped, and the fifteen-foot gilded electric gates didn't work. Diana was dying. It wasn't up to me to kill off her gallant myth that she still lived in a £1-million film set, like Cecil B. de Dors.

Now Newsdesk asked me to ring Alan Lake about the house sale. 'Sorry, but it has to be done, and it'll hurt less from you,' they lied, as must all newspapers to get what they want.

I rang Alan at 1 p.m. At 1.30 his housekeeper heard the gunshot which reunited him with the woman without whom he couldn't live.

On my first call to Sunningdale, a voice I instantly recognized as Alan's said, 'Mr Lake will be out this afternoon.' And he put the phone down. I rang back at once and said 'Alan, it's Rookie.' (I detest the nickname 'Rookie', but Diana had always used it, and only with her, I let it slide.) He replied, 'Yes, yes, dear, go on.' Then he said, 'I'm sorry, I'm in a bit of a state. It's a bad day today, a very bad day. It's the day I met her.'

I tried to buck him up with, 'Did you have your answering service on – what's all this stuff about "Mr Lake will be out this afternoon"?'

In a very firm, changed voice he said, 'Everything's going on here today. It's bedlam here today.'

Apart from his housekeeper, he was alone in the house.

'Look, I'm sorry I picked such a rotten day,' I said, 'but I see you're selling the house and I wondered if you could talk to me about it.'

A long silence. Then, 'Yes, Rookie. . . .'

'When will it suit you?' I asked.

'Wednesday,' he said. 'Next Wednesday will be OK.'

I asked, 'What time? – I'll fit in with you.'

'I can't think now,' he said.

'Look, Alan, forget it,' I said.

'No, I want to talk to you. Let's do it next week. It's the house, Rookie, I can't stand the house. I keep expecting her to walk in.'

I knew what he meant. Diana was everywhere. The phone was within eye-shot of her life-size portrait, in the days when her waist was a wedding ring. Except for her favourite gold lamé dress in which she was buried, her clothes were still in the wardrobes, along with whole chorus lines of high-heeled, peep-toed, ankle-strap shoes. One end of the living room was dominated by the ten-foot video screen on which, since her death, Alan had played and re-played her last programme for TV-am, in which she could still tell him, smiling from the screen, 'There's a lot of life in old Dors yet. I know I'm going to get well.'

'Alan, I'm so sorry I picked today,' I said. 'I'm so sorry about everything.'

'It's all right,' he said. Then in a low, choked voice, 'Goodbye, Rookie darling, goodbye.'

He put down the phone for no doubt the last time. And cut himself off from the world. I've always believed I disturbed him when he was on the precise point of taking his life. For Jason's sake, I've often wished I'd rung him back yet again. But I know it wouldn't have made any difference. The best of him had died, five months before, of a broken heart. No-one could have prevented him joining Diana. Mr Lake had been determined to be 'out this afternoon'.

For all of us involved, 1984 had indeed been what Diana forecast as 'the summer of my life, with a vengeance!' . . . And now, four years later, I too had cancer.

I became obsessed by the memory of her gallant losing battle to live. As the torment of the radiotherapy grew hotter, and the comfort about the future colder – just as I'd been warned, I *was* convinced that 'this is all going wrong but they daren't tell me' – Diana began to haunt me. Not literally, with the 'banging doors and wailing cries' horror stories which workmen on her now derelict Sunset Boulevardish mansion sold to the entranced *News of the World*, under the headline banner, 'Diana Dors' Ghost Walks!!!' What chilled me now was her remembered sunny nature, her useless optimism. She'd been so sure she had cancer 'beaten', 'taped', 'licked', and all those jolly words people use when they suspect they've had it. Even on the eve of her third major operation she'd assured us, 'I know I'm stronger than this damned disease which makes me so angry – it's not just what it does to your body, but to the people who love you.'

I didn't mind having a shot at the 'positive thinking' about which people who've never had cancer never stop yapping. But surely I was just pushing my luck, as Diana had, by twisting Fate's ear with all this 'positive' self-deception that I could be cured. When I actually reached the paranoid point of turning her framed letter to the wall, I wailed to the radiotherapist that I wanted to die *now*, and a nuisance to nobody, rather than be gradually hacked down like Diana. He slapped me down for playing Camille. 'All I know about

Diana Dors is what we all read in the papers,' he said. 'But she certainly didn't die of breast cancer.'

'She had a hysterectomy, a burst malignant ovarian cyst, and so much of her insides out she told me her stomach looked like "the scenic railway at Blackpool",' I admitted, feeling foolish.

'There's a hell of a difference, and, anyway, like everyone, she had a right to deal with cancer in her own way,' he rebuked me. 'Just because you're scared stiff, do you begrudge her the courage and hope she hung on to, right to the end?'

I don't begrudge dear old Di one gallant, glamorous lie to herself, I suddenly realized. And I wouldn't, for the world, have missed our last sunny day together at Sunningdale, when Diana opened the heart which, as usual, was practically exposed by the shocking neckline of her too-tight red and white polka-dot dress.

She had just heard that the cancer she'd 'beaten' for fifteen months had massed for another attack. Any other depressed woman would have been in the circular bed which could once make men's heads spin. Instead, she was lolling on it, lacquering her toenails scarlet – like Monroe and Jayne Mansfield she never wore tights or a girdle, summer or winter.

In the mirrors surrounding her, even on the ceiling, she reflected on her rich, full life, which had only three months left to run. She talked about her three husbands. Three sons. Silver screens, gold-plated sports cars. And wall-to-wall lovers once piled as thick as her fake fur carpets.

She was proud that, in her man-killing youth, Elvis Presley had queued for her, and not at the cinema. 'He was the best lover I ever had, the man was an earthquake,' she said, still jolted by remembered ecstasy. 'I was a damned fool not to marry him, instead of the three I did, but I never had any sense with men.'

Her first husband, Dennis Hamilton, died, at thirty-three, in a house-party fire which caused blazing world headlines. Her second, singer, Dickie Dawson, now an American chat show millionaire, left her with crippling tax problems which lost her the custody of their two sons, now twenty-nine and twenty-seven – who did not even come to her funeral.

And Alan Lake, ten years her junior, who was to commit suicide for her, had beaten her senseless, nightly, in the years before he beat the alcoholism which landed him in jail for a year on an assault charge. 'The biggest scene we ever had was when Alan shot the sofa, point blank, four times. Thank God he was so drunk he missed me, and riddled the cushions.'

At forty-two, she nearly died of meningitis – 'they told me I couldn't last the night.' At forty-four, she gave still, cruel birth to a beautiful eight-month-old boy. 'Alan saw him, but I couldn't bear to look.'

She recalled that, when they told her she had cancer, 'I said to the specialist "No, no, you've got it wrong, I'm not the cancer type."'

'If ever you get it, God forbid, the important step is to call it "cancer",' I remembered her telling me. 'Once you've said it, it stops being a dirty word.' How right she was, I knew now. There's nothing more irritating to a cancer patient than hushed-voice friends who stick at 'your operation', or worse still, 'the Big C', as if you'd just bought a ranch in Arizona. Cancer, by any other, frillier name, is as annoying as people who call death 'passing over' or 'on'.

I had asked her outright if she didn't feel at her tether's end at the recurrence of the disease which could end the brilliant career, as a character actress, she had built on the ruins of her film-star figure.

'If you mean, when they told me I'd got it again, was I furious with God, I was. All that praying, and now this,' she said. 'But then again, I may have been a wicked old so-and-so in my heyday, but I honestly don't think God would punish me for my past, so I still have faith. Or do you mean am I afraid of dying?' she asked, grinning at me over her Flame Red nail lacquer bottle.

I was almost afraid to nod. 'Yes, of course I am, especially in the middle of the night,' she said. 'I love life, whatever it's dished out to me. I love it so much that, even when I feel like death, I still come up for more every morning, like a buttercup.

'And you have to see the funny side of everything,' said the woman who, somehow, always did. 'When the cancer specialist told me I'd got it again, he said I was a very brave lady – I'm not, I'm scared stiff. Then he tried to cheer me up by kissing me. All I could think was, "God, he wants to be the last man who kissed Diana Dors."'

'But if only I could survive this next lot,' she said. 'It gave other women such hope when I beat the flab on TV-am – I lost fifty-two pounds, one for every year of my life. Just think what I could do for others if I proved you can beat cancer.'

'And if not?' I ventured, as the sun set in her bedroom mirrors.

'If not, then this must be a test to see if old Dors, at the end, really warrants eternal life,' she smiled.

Facing my own test, I trusted that Diana had Eternity now. And that those naturally golden-haired angels, who had never fallen, had not found old Dors lacking.

When we parted that day for what I knew, and she would never admit, was the last time, she gave me a second-hand rose silk dress. 'Wear it for me and enjoy it,' she said. 'And don't stitch the front up, it's supposed to plunge.'

Since her death, I'd never even touched it. Now I took it from its tissue paper, and tried it on. For the first time since the operation, I would see how far the lumpectomy would let me go. Tentatively, I pulled the neckline lower. Lower still. Long before I reached my scar, I was showing a Dors amount of untouched, still intact cleavage.

I grinned at myself in the full-length mirror I thought I could never face again. At that moment, finally, I knew that I must never forget Diana Dors. But pull myself together, shake off her golden dust, and get on with my life. . . .

CHAPTER ✦ SEVEN

A Lioness Among
the Tigers

*I*f I'd to choose between being caged with two man-eating tigers, and working for Sir Larry Lamb, I'd take the tigers.

I was on holiday in Sicily when Lamb the Legendary, Fiend of Fleet Street, took over the *Express* editorship in April 1983. Mount Etna was erupting at the time. It was an apt symbol of the mutual dislike which was to boil between me and Lamb for the next three flaming years.

'I thought I'd better warn you before you walk in on Monday and find him sitting there,' said Nicky forlornly over the poolside phone, as I stood, dripping with disbelief, watching distant Etna spit blood-coloured flames.

I had met Lamb once, ten years previously, when he'd tried to buy me for Rupert Murdoch's *Sun*. Since he offered no more money than I was already getting, but made it clear that the mere opportunity of working for him was in itself priceless, I turned him down. He was personally outraged. And I knew he was a man who had a long memory for being rejected.

Should I send him an allegoric postcard of Etna, or just wait for the inevitable explosion once I got back? It came within hours. 'So you're working for me after all. Everything comes to him who waits, love,' said a very cold Lamb on our first morning. By that afternoon we were flinging hot fat.

To be fair to Sir Larry – which I don't find easy – the fault lay in our stars, from birth. We were both bluntly, bloody-mindedly Yorkshire. It takes one to know one, and to me he appeared a quarrelsome, egotistical old Ilkley moorland ram. He was that most irritating of our kind, the truly professional Yorkshireman. As bloody awkward as Boycott, whom he idolized. He prized his knighthood and, working on one of Murdoch's Australian papers, brass-plated it to his door until some Crocodile Dundee on his staff scratched out the 'Sir' and replaced it with something very unmatey. But he affected the Yorkshire miner's son with a very black accent which left smuts on everybody he had a go at.

Lamb could scare a lion witless by lying down with it. Physically, he was a six-foot-four-inch, fifteen-stone Goliath, built, as they say where he and I come from, 'like a brick shithouse'.

Unarguably blindingly brilliant as the founder editor of the 'Soaraway *Sun*', Lamb believed that he could fly through the sun without his wings dropping off. He expected everyone to revolve around him, and detested stars on his paper. Only sycophantic satellites were allowed to form his close circle.

My column is not sacred, and I can be a bit of a cow. But, by this time, my *Express* page had been published as written, for a decade, by six satisfied editors. And for a logical reason. The column is a big Wednesday seller. They were paying me a whack to do it my way. So why, just for the sake of ruffling my feathers, rough up the Rook that lays the golden egg?

Back comes my first column for Lamb, with the speed of a boomerang, and clamped with a yellow sticker. He spread around yellow stickers 'From the Editor's Desk' like jaundice. On it were scribbled rewrite instructions, and not even from God Himself but from one of his disciples down the line.

I blew into Lamb's office like a blast from *Wuthering Heights*. Heathcliff was ready for me. 'I shall bloody well send my instructions down to you through anyone I like, and you'll bloody well do as I say,' he said, very quietly. Lamb had this theory that whispering like a breeze through a harebell when he was being really nasty had far more impact than roaring like a Force Eleven gale.

He was right. He'd put the wind up me. But I was damned if I'd bow down and snap at his first whistle. 'It's bloody well in my contract that I take my instructions on serious column changes directly and only from the editor,' I zapped back.

Lamb rose and towered above me like Michelangelo's Last Judgement. 'I'm asking you to leave my office, love,' he breathed in a very still, small voice that would have unnerved Moses. 'You're *what?*' I said. 'I'm *telling* you to leave my office this moment, Miss Rooooook!' he roared like a whirlwind, his eyes blazing from the vortex.

I should never have laughed. But you don't expect modern, hi-tech editors to utter such Victorian 'never darken my doors again' threats as they point you towards the snowstorm. Snorting with mirth, I cracked up. I thought Lamb was going to need the heart by-pass he in fact had three years later. When he turned the colour of moorland heather I realized he was serious. Emily Brontë wrote this bloke's script.

You don't go over editors' heads, however much you yearn to decapitate them. You can bang down your fist on the news, pictures, features, sports and foreign desks. You can eat the deputy editor alive for lunch. But any journalist who attempts to buck the editor – where the buck must stop – has no right to be in our business. So I would get out before Lamb and I carved each other up. Without stopping to think or blink at the imminent death of my career, I flew upstairs to the management, scrawling a shorthand note of my notice as I ran.

Lord Matthews, then Chairman of Express Newspapers, may have been cruelly dubbed 'Lord Whelk' by *Private Eye* because of his East End origins, but he was a fair boss and a streetwise politician. He informed me and Sir Larry, through a third party, that he wanted me to stay. I informed Lord Matthews, through the third party, that I would be sorry to go. Ever perverse Sir Larry informed the third party that he wanted me to stay, but that he wouldn't be 'buggered about'. Lamb's definition of being 'buggered about' was any black sheep on his staff who dared say 'baaah' to him, instead of 'Yes sir, yes sir, three bags full.'

What did I want from Sir Larry to stay on? inquired the management. His head on a silver platter, with mint sauce. But I'd settle for an apology.

For a week Lamb and I cut each other dead with sharpened carving knives. Then, three minutes before I was leaving one evening, Lamb's secretary issued me with a sort of social subpoena to appear at the Savoy for drinks. I swear Lamb had noticed, at that morning's conference, that I wasn't really dressed for the American Bar, and planned to catch me on the wrong, flat-heeled foot.

Fortunately for me, Sir Larry had soon got absolutely sauced. And by the time he was pickled as the white onions he insisted the Savoy must 'go out and buy' (at 7 p.m., in the Strand) because he fancied one, he in fact became intensely amusing. If I wasn't to lose my head, I must keep it now. I matched Sir Larry tomato juice for triple Scotch until I was swishing like the inside of a cold hot water bottle. The eighth time he told me, and everyone within booming distance, 'I *never* bloody apologize,' I took it as read, and promised to write off our differences, and write on.

As Sir Larry, with dangerously listing majesty, swayed across the Savoy's foyer, his eye caught some very small, prickly, ridiculously expensive roses in the flower shop. 'I wonder if any daft bugger ever buys these things,' he snapped thornily. The flower shop girl looked stabbed. 'I will present you with a rose, Miss Roooooook,' he said, paying an average man's day's wages for a cellophane coneful. In the back of his air-conditioned, telephoned Jaguar, he sniffed one. 'Plastic bugger!' he yanked off its head, 'I'd rather have buttercups myself.'

'Yes,' I said, momentarily carried away to our own county by his deep, harsh Yorkshire accent. 'Wouldn't it be great if they were wild Yorkshire flowers?' His eyes flamed like Heathcliff's. 'That's just it!' he enthused. 'Wild flowers with

85

bloody great bumble bees on 'em!' Maybe he's not such a bad stick after all, I thought, as we parted. At next morning's hung-over conference I realized I was wrong.

Of all the bilious yellow stickers he slapped on nearly everything I wrote, I received one note of primrose praise, for describing Coronation Street's Vera Duckworth as having 'a head like a brass bedknob, a voice like rusty springs, wire Brillo pad hair, and sex appeal so durable she could drop on a man like a five-feet-ten-inches, eleven-stone candlewick bedspread, and smother him with more than kisses.' Larry loved that. But still detested me.

Lamb's sudden fall-out with Lord Matthews, later divorce from Lord Stevens, and final crash from Express Newspapers, made the Roman Empire sound like a dropped pin. After The Fall, he became a newspaper consultant. Many months later I was told that in one of his reports Lamb had written, 'A successful newspaper depends on its regularly read stars – Jean Rook, for instance, is invaluable to the *Daily Express*.' Good old Heathcliff, the bad bugger. Spade-blunt and awkward to the last I heard of him, thank God.

Of my eight *Express* editors – Ian McColl (1971–4), Alastair Burnet (1974–7), Roy Wright (1977), Derek Jameson (1977–80), Arthur Firth (1980-1), Christopher Ward (1981–3), Larry Lamb (1983–6), Nicholas Lloyd (1986–) – Lamb left the deepest mark on me. I bear three scars – my Caesarian, my lumpectomy and Larry Lamb.

Alastair Burnet left a hallmark as distinguished as his silver hair. He was shatteringly glamorous, and, as seen on TV, a thrilling figurehead. From day one, he hated the job almost as much as we loved him. Alastair was a whizz with politics, cricket and the racing results. But useless on fashion, pop, and a national daily's daily grind of rapes, murders and disasters.

His ideal *Express* would have read like the *Week in Westminster* crossed with *Sporting Life* and *Wisden*. As the former editor of the *Economist*, he really didn't know what to do with a pacey, crumpled, inky, broad-based popular newspaper. When in doubt, as he frequently was, he'd vanish like a genie into the

Scotch bottle, invite half the staff to join him, and then pull in the cork.

Nothing became Alastair like his leaving of the *Express* which, for sheer style, made Fleet Street history. Editors who leave, or who are forced to, not only stick out for the golden handshake. If they could, they'd nick the silver spoons from the boardroom. Alastair staggered the management by refusing to be paid out even on his contract, because he himself was dissatisfied with his own handling of the job.

At his leaving party, there wasn't a dry eye or tongue in the packed office. In the decade since he left us, I've never heard even a whispered word against the most courteous, well-liked editor it was ever my joy to work for, and still call a close loyal friend. Even before the Queen's sword touched him, Sir Alastair was a 'parfit, gentil knight'.

Because he sounds like an overturned barrow in an East End gutter full of damp cabbage leaves, people initially judge Derek Jameson to be as thick as a shorn-off plank. In fact, Jameson was a brilliant, intuitive editor. As well as a one-man Palladium show. At Jameson's editorial conferences, you couldn't get a word in edgewise among his endless streams of jokey chat. Every morning, we just sat there for an hour, with our mouths open to no avail, listening to what was to become Radio Two.

Like Lamb, Jameson was farcically conceited. But, unlike Lamb, his egotism was never offensive. Self-confidence and self-congratulation simply oozed naturally from Derek, who often referred to himself in the third person: 'Did you ever 'ear about the time when Jameson . . . ?' Derek loved and admired himself. And would sit listening to himself, gasping with wonder.

He was pitifully upset when *Private Eye* dubbed him 'Sid Yobbo', and still won't accept that he'd only himself to blame for his Yobbohood. If an editor flashes his East End like a Pearly King, and forever rabbits on about his half-Jewish, half-starved Cockney grandmother, *Private Eye* is not going to wink at it. But, as an editor, Jameson was inspirational, and ran the paper like a knees-up at which everyone, from the highest to the lowest office boy he himself once was, was invited to join in the fun.

My own memorable experience of his shrewd, brilliant editorship came one afternoon when a planned US trip, for which we'd slotted 'Rook Round America' TV advertising, had dropped to bits the same morning. Two US politicians and three showbiz stars had all suddenly had to cancel interviews out of the blue – into which I was now flying 3,000 miles next day, with nothing set up. Since you can't waste thousands of the firm's profits on spec, I'd have to cancel.

'Cancel the trip? No' a' all. Lemme tell you the stories I wanna to 'ear from America,' said Derek, sounding more than usually worse than Max Bygraves. 'I wanna know what 'appens to people in New York who've been mugged so many times they 'aven't stepped out of their apartments for years – get a police car to 'Arlem and find out. Then I wanna know about these Born Again Christian telly preachers who rip off the viewers for thousands of dollars. And, while you're at it, why not spend a night in a San Francisco gutter with all the 'ippies and junkies and poofters?'

He shot off at least six more noisy, colourful ideas, without apparently even stopping to think. Between dodging broken bottles, inflamed Born Again Christians, and, at 2 a.m. in Harlem, actual non-blank bullets, it was the best American series I was lucky to live to write.

After surviving herds of editors, crashing through the *Express* to their doom at the average rate of one every two tempestuous years, I've become immune to danger. In fact I've sometimes deliberately flirted with fear.

Before Eddie Kidd hit the big time as the Levi advert's laundrette lethario, peeling off his 501s in front of millions of nakedly emotional teenage TV viewers, he was a motorcycle stuntman who had jumped fourteen double decker buses, twenty-three cars, twenty lions, ten disc jockeys, a 145-foot railway cutting. . . . And me.

I was younger and even more foolish then, and Eddie was

the nineteen-year-old Cockney Kid who made Evel Knievel look like a garden frog. When I fired the paper with the idea of interviewing Everready Eddie in depth, and height, colleagues enthused, 'The ideal picture would be of Kidd soaring over your head.' When I later produced the spectacular shot Eddie and I set up in an Essex quarry, strong sub-editors dropped the picture with a crashing cry of 'My God, we never meant you to actually *do* it!'

The Kidd's impact on a woman was flattening, even without his bike. He strutted a panther's physique, black hair glossy as his groin-tight leather pants, and cats' eyes you could have set into a motorway. In those innocent, pre-Levi days, before his zooming private life hit the headlines, the lovable lad had manners like beautifully polished wing mirrors.

Before he scared the living daylights out of me by clearing my hair-do with just enough daylight to spare, he took me aside. 'Would I 'urt you?' he purred into my trembling ear. 'Come off me bloody bike first, wouldn't I? And, even if my engine cuts out and I drop off the ramp at one mile an hour, I'll still travel ten feet, and just miss you.' I bet Harvey Smith says that to all the showjumping fences.

After an agonizing twenty-minute dry run, with a yard brush sitting in for me on a camp stool, Eddie was ready. The magnificent man on his flying machine revved up for the ramp. The quarry roared into life. Dry-lipped, and ash-grey as the coming clouds of dust, I contemplated death. The whizz Kidd who got his start by lining up eleven schoolmates, and leaping his pedal bike over them, may have jumped nine hundred times without breaking anything but records, but there was always the 901st. And how would they explain to Gresby, then eight, that his mother died when a man jumped on her from a great height, with sixteen stones of Yamaha attached?

I couldn't see Eddie for dust, not that I dared turn an eyeball. What was first a distant, summer gnat's wail swelled to a jaguar roar, then to a DC10, then Eddie hit the ramp like Concorde clouting the sound barrier, as all hell ('Don't stand *up*!' shrieked my brain, within inches of his back wheel) split and thundered loose above my head. Eddie had been, and gone, with the wind that made my hair, now stiff and white with quarry dust, stand on end. Years later, he told me I was hopscotch compared with the Grand Canyon.

I'm not sure which was more awesome – driving a Ben Hur chariot, or interviewing Ben himself, Charlton Heston. . . .

It was sheer, head-tossing, foam-flecked madness on my part to bet an Italian stunt team, at the 1983 Royal International Horse Show, that I could drive their Roman chariot. Especially since their four-horse-power, iron-wheeled Chariot of Fire could touch forty-five miles an hour on the flat out. 'What have you driven before?' asked the derisively snorting Italians. A pony and trap and a hard bargain, I said. I'd bet you my shirt and my life I can pinwheel round that arena like Boadicea or the Fifth Horsewoman of the Apocalypse.

Ben Herself.

The latter-day Romans stamped a bit, sweated buckets, and then, tempted by the leg-up of appearing all over the *Express*, assured one another it would be all right so long as I kept my head and the horses'.

What fazed me more than their snorting steeds was the startlingly small size of my fiery, blood-red painted chariot. How did they cram six-foot-five-inch Charlton Heston into something the size of an upturned fireman's helmet? 'Don't worry about the size, it's more difficult to turn over than it looked in *Ben Hur*,' said the stuntmen. They were wrong. The very night after my historic race, their chariot overturned, a wheel flew off into the crowd, and the Horse Show called a halt to the entire, neck-breakingly dangerous act. Depending how you view the show that was banned on British TV as too dangerous, I was lucky to get in there before the crash.

What my chariot lacked in size was made up for by the slaughterous charm of my thirty-five-year-old Italian charioteer, name of Mario. 'You will appear to be alone in the picture, but insurance makes it necessary for me to crouch in the bottom of your chariot, holding your legs,' he leered. Any woman who willingly exposes her legs to an Italian crouching under her crotch is dicing with worse than death, even before the off.

Mario directed that the art of looking like a Roman frieze – mane and hooves flying, neck and nostrils stretched – was to stiffen your courage with your spine, lie back on the reins, and think of the Colosseum. By now his Four Horses, gleaming black and Apocalyptic, were champing at the foaming bit. Holding a handful of spaghetti-reins, I felt magnificent as living sculpture. What did I have to do to make these updated bronze statues actually move?

'You must give them definite instructions, but not in English, because they are pure Andalucian, and do not scream whatever,' snorted Mario hotly.

'*Quo Vadis?*' I said, desperately.

'Girrup!' enthused Harvey Smith, who'd strolled over to watch.

'*Allez!*' bawled Mario.

With a crack of sixteen thunderous hooves, everything broke loose – the reins, buckets of sweat, my spine and rattling teeth. As we flew round the bend at thirty miles an hour, Mario shouted: 'Wait until we get back on the flat!'

On the flat, I was nearly out. It was a Roman orgy of wild, barbaric, roaring, dust-choked ecstasy and agony, with legs, arms, hooves, me, Mario, and everything exquisitely entwined. The whole reeling scene was choked with passionate dust. 'Having you ever experienced anything like that?' exulted Mario, bringing it all to a panting, shuddering, perspiration-soaked stop. Nothing I could ever print.

It was mercifully after I'd completed the ride I met Mario's trainer, the elderly Paris-born Bernard Celeyron, who actually trained the eighty horses used in the film *Ben Hur*. Hobbling on two sticks – 'I have more injuries than I can count' – Monsieur Celeyron gave me every cough, spit and near death-rattle describing a stuntman who fell in the filmed chariot race, and nearly severed several parts of himself from life.

Was he telling me that Charlton Heston, in sweating,

anguished, tangle-locked close-up, was actually driving Ben Hur's chariot? Discreetly, Monsieur Celeyron wasn't telling me.

So I asked Charlton Heston. 'Hell, no, I was towed by a Cadillac,' said Ben himself. 'You never actually drove one? What was it like?' Like being trapped in an empty washing machine or shooting Niagara Falls in an oil drum.

Which is how you feel after a face to face with Charlton Heston. The man is colossal. Monolithic. Panoramic. A cast of thousands in himself. I've never seen anything like him, apart from the Washington statue of Abraham Lincoln, Mount Rushmore, and a ninety-foot Japanese Buddha.

It's not just that the world's most epic film star is physically immense. He's completely removed. His face is hewn rock: his eyebrows overhang it, like cliffs: his cloud-splitting voice thunders from his summit, and, when he speaks, even his teeth are massive ivory tablets on which you could carve holy law.

'Call me Chuck, my friends do,' Heston urged me, the first time I met him, in 1976. The second time we met, in 1988, I still couldn't call him 'Chuck'. Even though, by this time, our all-time cosmic hero had lowered himself to play Jason Colby in that hairpiece that looked like a ginger tomcat squatting between the ears of a Trafalgar Square lion.

'I like Jason. I invented him. Jason was a good man who kept his promises and did his best,' said Mr Heston, who argues he gets fed up with everyone perching him as Moses on top of Mount Sinai, or Michelangelo stuck up the scaffolding of the Sistine Chapel. 'And why can't you call me Chuck?'

Because it would be like putting a pickle bottle label on a Holbein portrait, I said. And, anyway, in real life, off camera, I expected him to act the only big part he hasn't been offered on it. God.

'Oh, God, no,' he gasped, genuinely aghast. 'If you mean have I let playing three Presidents, two saints and a genius go to my head, I haven't. In normal life, I'm cheerful, trustworthy, energetic, professional and friendly.

'Of course I haven't been changed by my epic roles. I'm

not, for instance, formally religious. It would be presumptuous of me to say, "I played Moses, and found God!" Though you can't walk barefoot up Mount Sinai and come down quite the same as you went up.'

Surely his hair didn't really grow six inches and turn white? 'No, but if you scrape around inside the skulls of great people, it's bound to have its effect. If you give full measure, and for the enormous amounts of money you're paid I think you should, you really live the part.' Heston does. Even Brits who were prepared to carp that no man born in Illinois, who'd played that great block of soap, Jason Colby, could rise to *A Man For All Seasons*, were knocked out of their theatre seats by Heston's 1988 performance of Sir Thomas More.

A lot of cloudy myth has settled round his peak in sixty-three years. Like my information that the Goliath sculpted in flesh doesn't drink, smoke, swear, has no sense of humour, and lives on 250 vitamin pills a day. 'Where on earth did you get that from?' he gulped down shock with a double Scotch. From the film director who's supposed to have snorted of Heston, 'He's so pure he could cure the sick with a sneeze.'

What probably rattles lesser men, I explained – not to mention women who know they've no more chance of conquering Heston than Everest – is his rocklike forty-four-year-old marriage to Lydia, the college sweetheart he wed at nineteen. Is he an epic prude? I risked the wrath of the nearest Hollywood has got to God, by asking him had he never dropped one of those Ten Commandment tablets, and shot a woman a line that wasn't in the script?

And, if not, what was the secret of Eternal Married Life? 'Realizing you can't live in perfect bliss every minute of the day – no one can. What you've got to learn is not to think, when you squabble, "Oh God, that does it! I can't bear it!" You've got to surmount life's bumps. Always assume that the other person is doing his, or her, best – and be as ready to find excuses for that other person as you are to find them for yourself.'

Mr Heston seemed genuinely unaware that he'd just beautifully paraphrased a whole slab of the Sermon on the Mount.

And still pressed me to call him Chuck. From now until the Last Judgement, in which he'll probably have a plum part, I could never manage 'Chuck' without feeling that the earth could move, and the waters swallow me up. But at least I'd caught this living George Washington out in a little white lie that he'd 'taken chariot lessons' for the film in which he wasn't even an L-driver.

'I did stand in the firebucket, but, all right, I wasn't doing forty-five miles an hour. Neither were the stuntmen. Know how you can tell? Next time you watch that film galloping round and round, notice that you always see eight horses' heads, but not at the same time as you see the distance between the chariots' wheels,' Heston smiled, his teeth like Doric pillars in the noonday sun.

'But there's one thing I've done that I'm proud of, and nobody can deny it. I genuinely rowed that damned Ben Hur galley all the way home.'

Apart from taking on Larry Lamb, the wildest self-imposed test of my ability to keep my head in a crisis in which I could have literally lost it, was my face-to-fanged-face with a pair of Bengal tigers. The tigers weren't stuffed. Or rugs. Or posters for Esso. They were the real, woman-eating thing. The trick has never been performed by Fleet Street, before or since, and, if it had gone wrong, I'd have been bloodily splashed across my own front page, and probably made *News at Ten*.

When Mary Chipperfield, daughter of the grand old circus family, dared me to interview her in a cage with two fully grown tigers, vanity had me slobbering at a chance to be photographed, looking like the cat's whiskers, while actually standing directly under the cats' whiskers. I didn't know, before I met one, that a tiger has whiskers a foot long, shark's teeth, razor claws, weighs thirty-five stones, and can take off from a stool at thirty-five miles an hour. We are not talking about a king-size ginger tom in striped pyjamas.

My insurance was ferocious, and even the *Express* turned ivory with terror when I set up my appointment with fear and Miss Chipperfield. 'There's no real danger, so long as you keep your nerve,' soothed Mary, setting up two thumping great tigers on stools the size of dinner plates.

'We've worked it all out that, to get to you, they'd have to eat my father first, then a keeper, two cage attendants, and me last, in that order.'

Mary's father, Jimmy Chipperfield, wonderfully calm at being the first course on the menu, reassured me, 'After all our years in the circus, we're not going to risk the lot on a tiger harming you.' He didn't tell me until afterwards that his own father-in-law had been half-eaten to death, publicly, by a lion.

On the dreaded day, I turned up on Clapham Common, where the circus was staging a gala performance for Princess Anne. I had with me the *Express*'s chief royal photographer, Steve Wood, who dismissed this as a doddle compared with fighting off packs of rabid, rival cameramen on a royal tour of the US. He pointed out they were only man-eating tigers. Tame pussycats compared with snarling Prince Philip, in a spitting temper, cornered by the press. 'Anyway, you should be OK, I've just seen them fed,' Steve patted my now quivering flank. 'They seemed to be eating whole cows' heads.'

If what I was doing, if I did it, was so safe, I asked Mary, why do safari parks make so much of guns, warning notices, and electrified fences? 'Because, if you get out of your car, a tiger will have you in a flash,' she said. 'Lions in parks would wait until you're stuck right in front of them to eat you. Tigers are waiting all the time, looking like lovely pussies – with kids, that's the danger – for someone to stick a finger out of the window. They'll have it in a split second.'

So what are circus tigers? Toys, tranquillized, tired? 'They're exactly the same as safari tigers, they'd snatch you in a flash. The only difference is you've got me with you.'

By this time I had with me two trainers, two cage men, and Daddy Chipperfield with a pronged fork and a fire extinguisher. But where was his gun? 'What gun?' he snapped. 'You can't use guns, you'd kill the audience. People don't pay ten pounds for a box to get shot.'

In their outside cage, the tigers were yelling to get at

the Christians. When six of them streaked, like orange fire, through the tunnel of terror between their cage and the ring, I commended my spirit.

'Nothing can go wrong for you, but this is quite dangerous for us,' said Chipperfield, eyes narrowed and muscles rippling. 'Be prepared, once you're through those bars, for the tigers to look different. Much, much bigger – it will come as a shock. I don't think you'll panic, you're not the type, but if you do feel hysterical, just ask me very quietly to take you out. For God's sake and everybody else's, don't scream and run.'

The six tigers were playing ring-a-ring-a-Mary. At her whip crack, they sat upright and still on their stools, like identical petrol commercials. Another crack, and four were parted from my pair, and sent back through the tunnel. If we kept all six, I could be photographed right in the big middle, I said, with the courage of hysteria. 'Too risky,' said Chipperfield – I could end up in someone's big middle. 'Did you notice the face of one of those tigers we sent out – she's terribly dangerous.' Aren't they all? 'Yes, but she's special. She's got the tight face, the flat ears that spell real danger. Mary would know seconds before she turned nasty. You wouldn't.

'There's no such thing as a tame tiger, and anyone who thinks so is a fool, but your two are as near tame as you can get, and, while Mary's there, you'll be safe as houses. Ready?' he said, sounding like Nero.

'Ready!' I panted, feeling like Daniel. The cage opened a crack. Some idiot growled 'good luck'. I was on.

Seen through the bars, the tigers had looked like overweight tabbies. Now, as Chipperfield had warned, they filled the world from which they could swipe me with one paw. Slowly I walked towards them across the sawdust, my mouth as dry. Delhi and Bengal, looking exactly like William Blake's tiger, just sat there in their fearful symmetry. Burning a damned sight too bright for comfort.

Mary slipped me two sticks with meat on the end. 'Feed them,' she growled softly (God, what with, a leg?). 'With the meat, but both precisely at the same time, that's important. Now, raise both sticks, and shout "Allez-*oop*!" – loud.'

I raised my sticks like André Previn about to belt out Beethoven's Fifth with both hands. Then shouted the magic, childhood cry of the circus – 'Allez-*oop!*' Up went my tigers like striped escalators. They hung in the air, towering infernos, their eyes blazing, and all this was at my command. Power surged through me, and my blood (forget blood, forget it!) pounded with excitement. Compared with this mighty moment, Larry Lamb was but one of life's cold scraps.

Afterwards, the Great Chipperfield stroked my ego. 'You did well. I know a lot of strong men who wouldn't do what you've done today,' he said, as my thrilled ears twitched at his praise like a tickled tigress. 'And I could name you a lot of circus men who've actually sat outside that cage, longing to do it, but petrified, and sweating blood.'

How I needed to re-kindle those words as I daily walked past the radiotherapy department's warning sign NO ADMISSION BEYOND THIS POINT. And how often I told myself that cancer was just another non-paper tiger I had to face, and handle.

CHAPTER ✦ EIGHT

Tea with Taylor

I had waited thirty years to interview Elizabeth Taylor. She was my schoolgirl heroine, my teenage role model, and my age, dammit, to within three months. When she and I were twelve, I thundered with her over every fence of *National Velvet*. My pounding heart crashed with ecstasy through my green serge gymslip as, gripping Yorkshire cinema seats with my thighs, I re-watched that film galloping round and round.

When we were thirty-three, my envious soul rode with Taylor through wild nights of rearing, plunging passion with Richard Burton. I had fallen head over school sandals with Burton on a fifth form trip to Stratford on Avon, when he was twenty-two, I was seventeen, and Elizabeth Taylor had never been publicly kissed by anyone but Lassie. Playing Prince Hal in *Henry IV* like a slender, vibrating Welsh harp string, Burton had plucked on everything in me. As I craned from my 2s. 6d. seat in the gallery, my eyes steaming up my father's field glasses trained on my hero, I knew my first orgasmic desire.

That summer, I devoured, slept, and dreamed Burton. As my teens wore on, he never completely wore off. Years later,

I frayed cassettes and my emotions to tatters, mooning over his narration of *Under Milk Wood*. When he married Taylor first time round, in 1964, God and my unsuspecting husband would have to forgive me for a stab of evergreen jealousy.

I met Burton only once, thirty years after Stratford, on his honeymoon with Suzy, former wife of the racing driver James Hunt. I'd known Suzy since my *Daily Sketch* days when I gave her her first star modelling job at the Paris collections. And nearly lost my job when we discovered, in a Paris hotel, too late, that Suzy couldn't squeeze into the French fashions with a shoehorn.

Haute couture in those days was designed for bustless, bottomless, and apparently gutless French mannequins. Suzy Miller, soon to be Mrs Hunt, and later Mrs Burton, was tall as the Eiffel Tower, and a strapping size ten. Any man would have given ten out of ten to her uptilted boobs and spectacularly sexy behind. To be fair, when I vetted her photographic portfolio in London, and booked her for Paris, Suzy had a more accurate measure than I of her slim chances of squashing her voluptuous charms into a Dior dress made for a plank. 'I'm bigger than I look – I don't think you should risk it, much as I'd love to do it,' she flashed her panoramic smile above her Grand Canyon cleavage.

As a fashion writer, my sense of her proportion was blinded by the prospect of dazzling pictures of the *Sketch*'s blonde, boisterous sexy Suzy, after lean years of gaunt-ribbed, grim-faced French models. 'But what happens if we can't pack me inside the clothes?' she was still panicking on the flight to Paris.

We couldn't cram her inside anything. As we struggled, and failed, to shrink her into the garments, zips whined and buttons shot off like machine gun bullets. The strain on the seams and my photographer was killing.

There had to be a way round her. Doggedly, I bought dozens of heavy duty metal bulldog clips, and was forced to break my own rule not to fiddle physically with the model girls by unzipping the outfits down the back, and clamping them to her undies. Since Suzy's undies were scant, I pegged out so much flesh she began to look as if she'd been flogged.

Spooned and clipped into the skimpiest frocks, and photographed head on, she was stunning. But her rear view was so scandalous we were hounded off the Champs Élysées by shocked, if slobbering, gendarmes who suspected we were shooting *haute porn.* Compared with the usual pictures of the Paris houses' cat-walking corpses, our Sunshine Suzy, bursting with healthy radiance from the *Sketch*'s front page, was the season's sensation. She'd have caused even greater uproar if we'd published the rear views of her, splitting the skin-tight outfits like a part-peeled, five-feet-eight-inches banana.

Suzy and I stitched up a firm friendship as we unpicked Paris's seams. I was invited to the Hunt wedding, but couldn't go as I was abroad. By the time I got round to ringing Mrs Hunt to find out how her twenty-two-month-old marriage was going, it was all but gone out of the window through which Suzy claimed James hurled her packed suitcase at 140 m.p.h.

Next thing I heard, she'd gone for the Burton. So I rang the newly-weds at the Dorchester, where they were lying low and giving no interviews. I finally shoved my way past the hotel telephonist permanently blocking the line to the Burtons' suite with, 'Well, at least leave Mrs Burton my name!' Within seconds, Suzy was on the line. She would love to arrange a meeting between me and Richard, she enthused, snatching my half-formed request out of my mouth which was suddenly dry at the thought of meeting my girlhood's fantasy lover.

I warned myself that my crumbling idol's feet would be clay. In his hell-raising Hollywood years since my schoolgirl Stratford, whole rivers of vodka had roared under Burton's frequently tottering bridge. He would probably turn up tighter than his wife had looked in those long ago fashion shots.

Under the influence of nothing but Suzy, who had managed to jam a temporary cork in the legendary Burton boozing, my hero was stone cold sober, and warmly friendly. But Suzy looked sadly subdued. Damaged by the crash of her high-speed marriage to world champion Hunt, and nervously trying to steer her new marriage to the easily skidding Burton, she'd lost so much bounce and weight she could have slipped through a Dior dress without touching the sides. Her happiness, though still transparent, had a fragile quality. You knew, even from the start of their fated six-year marriage, it could only be a matter of time before she snapped, and he blew his Dom Perignon cork.

My meeting with Burton was vintage, over a bone-dry BBC lunch at the studio in which he was recording the narrative for a radio series. Shamelessly unscrewed with excitement, I lightheadedly poured out my bottled-up teenage worship, like a libation at my idol's feet. This was wine to his loosened tongue, which began spouting jetting crystal fountains of Shakespeare and Dylan Thomas. For three enchanted hours, I had to myself the voice which had disturbed my virgin sleep. Chipped and battered as my idol was, he was still the Burton the Beautiful I had tried to touch with my binoculars. Older, greyer, sadder, but not, one suspected, wiser, he still vibrated like a harp and, though already sinking towards his sunset, momentarily gleamed like the young Prince Hal, holding up the golden crown.

I never saw Burton again, off-screen. When he died of a drink-induced brain haemorrhage in 1984, I didn't mourn the fallen international star. I grieved for the lost and wasted actor – the Welsh miner's genius son with the pitted face and the one-man Eisteddfod voice, ringing like chapel bells across the valleys.

My childhood god was gone. Now, at last, I was to meet his eternal goddess, Elizabeth Taylor, the woman with – or without – whom the ever-besotted Burton could not live.

I'd actually seen Taylor, a dozen years ago, and initially from afar, at a Paris party. My instant reaction was: 'Looking like that, how the hell does she do it? Why, at her age, can't I do it? And why have five husbands (her count at the time) fallen for it?' For that tubby little figure across the room which was crowded by the size of her hips? She was squat and broad-beamed as an overpainted Russian doll, and, if you could have lifted her, you'd have expected to find half a dozen more dumpy, wooden Elizabeth Taylors slotted inside.

Then, for a brief, passing nod, I was introduced. Close up, the face was fabled. Suddenly you knew why it had launched a fleet of marriages, and why strong men gladly drowned in the fathomless violet lakes of her eyes.

An excusive, no-holds-barred, two-hour interview with Taylor is as rare as her Krupp diamond, and trickier than a house of cards to set up. It takes months on the phone and paper to build up her agents' and entourage's confidence. It takes La Liz a mere whim to change her mind and everyone else's overnight, and tear up the deal with one tiny, imperious hand.

The *Express* had paid £100,000 for Taylor's sensationally revealing book on her battle with booze, drugs and obesity, *Elizabeth Takes Off*, on condition that she gave us a one-to-one interview. I was asked to write what had to be a newspaper bestseller.

Pinning Taylor down was like trying to drink tea out of the Holy Grail. Through the autumn and winter of '87, she gave me the slip from day to day, and country to country, in which she would/wouldn't/might be filming. My calendar was as black with cancelled dates as I was with frustrated fury at the wayward woman.

Cancer for Christmas cut Taylor, and everything else but my immediate survival, from my mind. I was barely into radiotherapy when the *Express* rang, on New Year's Day, to tell me my interview was set firm, no backsliding, for 3 p.m. on 1 February. Did I still want to do it? I was touched by the way they put it. 'Do you still want to?' restored so much more of my carved-up confidence than 'Are you sure you'll be able to?' or the 'Are you sure you'll still be around to?' which must have crossed their minds.

Yes, I still wanted to. After thirty years, nothing would prevent that historic 3 p.m. appointment but the Last Trump sounding at 2.55.

What I hadn't foreseen was that 1 February would dawn during the last flaming week of my radiotherapy, when my skin and all hell of depression would be breaking loose. As things at the cancer hospital hotted up, my courage cooled. By the end of the month, even Alan Frame's confidence was beginning to shake like my exhausted voice on the phone, though he only asked, bless him, too casually and too often, if I was sure I was up to it?

So physically and mentally down I could have crawled under a snake without disturbing it, I desperately tried to keep up my end of the phone. I was fine. Well, not five star, but still star writer enough to insist they didn't pass on Taylor to anyone else.

On the eve of the great day, I was burning up in my bed of what now felt like live coals, when the *Express*'s TV advert blazed across my screen. 'THE WAR OF THE WIDOWS!!!' it hectically shrieked. 'Read Jean Rook's exclusive interview, only in the *Daily Express*.'

War of what widows??? And what chump in our advertising department had omitted to warn me they expected me to mention Sally Burton to a livid Liz, who would probably kill me long before cancer? Steaming with rage, I rang the *Express* to demand what they thought they were doing, and how the hell did they expect me to do it?

'It was such a dramatic plug for your series. . . .'

'Series?' I interrupted.

'Yes, haven't we mentioned we want to run you three days instead of one? Well, like we said, it was such a good plug we thought you'd be thrilled with it,' they trailed off miserably, and then cunningly perked up with, 'The editor wrote it.'

'The bloody editor doesn't have to face Liz Taylor with it,' I seethed, plunging back between my sizzling sheets. I tried to switch off my boiling thoughts, but my simmering nerve had gone. Next morning, dried out and burnt through, I tried to crawl out of my infernal pit. My white fake-fur bedroom carpet suddenly changed into a polar bear, sprang at me, and hurled me to the floor. When my mother found me, the coffee cup she'd brought clattered in its saucer. 'I don't think you can make it,' she said, losing her head for the first time since I'd mentioned cancer. 'You'll kill yourself.'

'There'll be no need if I ring the *Express* at this late date and cry off, they'll do it for me,' I said.

I wasn't over-reacting. Not only was my name on the ticket in huge print, with 'THE WAR OF THE WIDOWS!!!' raging on TV-am since 7a.m.; but for six weeks I'd behaved like a bitch in the manger, snappishly snarling at any suggestion that another member of the staff, who were all slobbering for it, should take over the job.

The only precaution I'd taken was to insist her publishers warn Liz Taylor what was the matter with me, since, in fairness to her, I couldn't risk inexplicably falling down or throwing up on the job. In my immediate condition, flat on my haggard, unmade-up face, such foresight seemed nit-picking.

An hour and three coffees later, I was on my feet, swaying like a ragged scarlet poppy in a gale. And worrying: how was I going to squeeze my scorched and tattered boob into a Tea with Taylor outfit? Desperately scouring my wardrobe for a sack which didn't look too much like one, I came up with a mistake I'd made on a rather tiddly late-night shop in Las Palmas – a sort of denim clown suit with elasticated ankles and a ballooning top. I looked like an overweight Colombine, or Pagliacci struggling to see the funny side of it. I was hugely bucked later when Liz Taylor, string-thin at the time but always with an eye for a tent to hide in, enthused, 'God, that is a *great* outfit! – *Where* did you get it?'

My limo driver was the same one who had brought me back from London after my operation. Of course I looked all right, he lied gamely, I should have seen myself six weeks ago, he said, as he dropped me at the Dorchester.

Taylor's right hand woman and confidante for seventeen years, Chen Sam, an exotic Oriental with the upswept topaz eyes and lithe body of a sacred cat, undulated down to say Elizabeth would be a little late. As one of the journalists who'd waited two hours, the previous summer, for Taylor's triumphal, Cleopatra-scale entry at the Cannes Film Festival, I thought at least an hour's heel-cooling curtain raiser was standard Taylor tactics. Not this time. In washing her hair,

Elizabeth had blown every chandelier on the Dorchester's penthouse floor, so the breakdown was genuine.

The fifty-minute wait for the Grand Entrance was anguish. I felt lousy, my adrenalin was dropping by the minute, my small talk had dried up like my mouth, and a few sips of lemon tea had disagreed sourly with my radiotherapy. Please God, smite me later, but don't let me fall down and chuck up at Taylor's feet.

The Second Coming I was braced for was surprisingly low key, as La Living Legend emerged from the bathroom, her just-lacquered hair a spiked black chrysanthemum, tipped with silver. At this time of the publication of her blockbusting bestseller, Taylor's physical impact, at eight-and-a-half stones, had more breath-stopping clout than ever it had at thirteen-and-a-half. She was so Dresden tiny, you could have lost her among the porcelain *objets* on the hotel suite's mantelpiece.

The woman was reborn. Her no-longer-broad bosom delicately swelled under a clinging black-edged white wool sweater. Her hips in sleek black pants were less than half the size of 'those monstrous thighs' she had spent months of misery dieting into the pair of too-tight jeans she daily tried on, like a penitential hair shirt. The fabled eyes which had 'disappeared into suet – just lost in huge bowls of fat', were once again prize purple pansies. Even her rather scratchy screen voice – at her worst, Taylor sounds on film like Virginia Woolf on a hot tin roof – was way down to a new, all-time low girlish whisper.

She was as open as her book. The most gripping passage in *Elizabeth Takes Off*, which finds an echo in the over-broad bosom of every middle-aged, spreading woman, describes how, after five fat years of 'speeding past full-length mirrors', and 'making up my face in bits so I never saw the disastrous, triple-chinned whole', she took herself in hand. Literally. Roll by roll of surplus flesh.

The full-length mirrors in our Georgetown home were in the dressing room behind doors which were generally closed. I had planned it that way. But this one day I got out of the tub, made myself open the closet doors, and saw myself, my entire self.

I saw the shape I was in and I could not believe it, I was obese.

I could not tear myself away from this awful vision, and, at the same time, I could not help superimposing on it the young woman I had been, the eager teenager in *National Velvet*, the seductive wife in *Cat on a Hot Tin Roof*, the noble temptress in *Cleopatra* – but the longer I stared the longer I was confronted with the dreadful truth.

I was no longer one of the most beautiful women in the world, and, much worse, I was no longer Elizabeth Taylor, the person I knew.

No woman, let alone a blazing star, has so totally stripped and humbled herself in the eyes of her fellow women. She herself, she told me, chose the book's terrifying, ton-weight *before* pictures which made her look heavy enough to smash a coffee table. 'Even the publishers said, "Those pictures are really ugly, you don't have to be so hard on yourself", but I had to be cruel to myself if I was going to peel right down and put it over to other people.'

Where did she find the guts to spill them, I asked her, and, naked, was she really the hideous Titanic Taylor she made herself look in print? 'I was worse,' she admitted to me simply. 'You saw my chins, those great dewlaps that practically met my breasts. The rest of my obese body was just mountains of fat,' she said. And she cracked me up with a story of how she'd recently stripped again, 'because I get so cheesed off with people who say it's all done with facelifts or suction or bits of plastic when, honestly, all I've had is a chin tuck to take up all those lost surplus chins. I got so pissed off with a friend who kept telling me beside her swimming pool to be honest about all the bits I've had "suctioned out" I ripped off all my clothes. She just stood there gasping: "I see, Elizabeth, thank you" . . .'

Her honesty about her stint in the Betty Ford Clinic was

staggering. 'I was at the bottom,' she told me, as she and I righteously nibbled nothing but the cucumber, at fifty pence a slice, I estimated, out of the Dorchester's swanky sandwiches. 'I knew I was pill addicted, I didn't know I was an alcoholic because I never got drunk. I loved the fact that I could drink anyone under the table – and that included Richard Burton,' she smiled at the first mention of the beloved name.

'When I got home, I took sleeping pills on top of the booze and walked into walls, but since nobody saw that, I didn't see it myself – just like the fat I wouldn't look at in the mirror. Since I was the first "celebrity" at the Betty Ford, they didn't know what to do with me – should they give me private sessions? But that wouldn't have worked out,' she said. 'Since I was like everybody else – lonely, in pain, in a mess – I had to go through the hot seat just like everybody else, and I knew it.

'The first night I stood up and said "My name is Elizabeth", and all the group shouted back, "Hi, Elizabeth!"' she said – perfectly imitating the high, piping, jolly voice of an American AA meeting – 'I just mumbled, "I'm a pill addict," and immediately sat down.

'The next night I suddenly got up the guts to stand up and say, "I'm Elizabeth, and I'm an alcoholic." I knew then that I could and would have to stand up to the group therapy where they peel off all the layers we all hide inside. It's like peeling an onion or taking away the cotton wool we all use to protect ourselves from life's sharp edges. Before they can cure you, they make you run into those sharp edges and feel the pain.'

I had visited the spartan Palm Springs clinic where the unhappy inhabitants make their own beds, and clean their own shared rooms, while they dry out and tip out their minds to others in torturous group therapy. It was light years from the £1,000-a-night pale green silk Dorchester suite with its transparent cucumber sandwiches. How could the great Hollywood star reveal she had fallen so low by eating self-service canteen meals, and getting down on her knees to scrub the corridor outside her small, bare, and not even private room?

'Because it wasn't Elizabeth Taylor doing the chores we all had to do as part of our recovery. It was the real me as I was then. A fat, confused, middle-aged woman who'd finally decided I must change my lifestyle if I wanted to live.'

Taylor didn't spare us a tearful drop of her psychological sufferings at the Betty Ford, or the pain of the rigid diet she began when she heard that her old rival, Debbie Reynolds – married before her to Eddie Fisher – had stuck one of Elizabeth's fat pictures on her refrigerator 'to remind herself not to look like me' Taylor winced. 'I thought "good idea, Debbie" – and stuck my own picture on my own fridge door.'

She was even able to smile, no longer 'laughing on the outside, and crying and dying on the inside', retelling some of Joan Rivers's endless stream of cruel Fat Liz jokes. 'I thought one of the funniest was "Elizabeth Taylor appeared in town today in a yellow dress. A party of school kids at a bus stop ran over and tried to board her,"' Taylor roared – the famous laugh, unlike the rest of her, was still full-bellied.

Since she's only a year older than Joan Collins, I asked why Taylor doesn't play games with toy boys. 'A boy of twenty-four when you're fifty-six could make you feel really insecure,' she grinned. 'That's when I really would start getting paranoid about wrinkles and how my thighs look in a swimsuit.'

When I probed her feelings for her frequent companion, Gorgeous George Hamilton, who shared Taylor's restored limelight when she burst on Cannes, looking slim as a single rose in a taffeta dress of flaming petals, she hooted, 'They told us to be late – but two hours! I guess I overdid it. God, I enjoyed that entrance, I felt like a kid again. But I know I'm not a kid any more,' she added serenely. 'I don't look as great as I did at twenty. I don't look anything like as pretty – well, quite pretty – as I looked as Maggie in *Cat on a Hot Tin Roof* at thirty-five. I look fifty-six. But I look like Elizabeth Taylor should look at fifty-six, that's what counts.

'As for George, I've no plans to marry him. He's set in his

ways, he has his life as he likes it. George is the perfect bachelor playboy, and I don't think I should spoil it.'

I couldn't warn her at the time, since I wasn't to meet him until four months later, that not even slimmed-down Elizabeth Taylor had the leanest chance of spoiling anything for spoilt, vain, but unarguably gorgeous and lovable George.

I was braced, like the corset I was convinced he wore, to detest the perma-tanned tailor's dummy of an actor, on whose permanently crooked arm Taylors, Collinses, Linda Evanses and Oxenburgs are pictured, clinging like helpless bits of fluff. Five minutes into our interview, I was deep as his tan in love with George. The six-feet-two-inches block of chocolate had melted me with his built-in sunshine.

In what you can't believe is flesh, Hamilton looks so sculpted in bronze, or carved from solid mahogany, you marvel he can move. His sideboards are silver, his eyes twenty-four-carat gold. He's so like something out of a Harrods display, you hesitate to invite him to sit down in case the knees in his creaseless trousers are not actually jointed. I jumped when he flashed his piano-key teeth, and cheerfully agreed, 'Sure, I look like something out of a shop window!

'I'm very vain, but it's a healthy vanity. Being vain doesn't mean I look in the mirror a lot. People who spend hours at the mirror are trying to cover up things, they're worried it's not going right. I believe in myself. I'm a good person. Women like me because I'm fun, I'm a good time, I bring sunshine into their lives,' said the man who has a two-month suntan clause written into his film contracts. 'Though you can catch sun anywhere in a sheltered spot, did you know that? I once crawled out on to the roof of a London hotel to grab a few little precious rays – next thing I knew I was looking down at twenty people waving and yelling at me not to jump.'

I asked was it true that he loves himself more than half Hollywood's female stars, forever draped round him? And does he really spend happy hours smirking at a life-size, long-after-Gainsborough oil painting of himself, tarted up like a Mills and Boon hero in crotch-tight breeches, and a white ruffled shirt slashed to the waist?

'I might if I still had it,' beamed the latter-day Apollo whom nothing ruffles. 'Some friends wanted to see it, so I stuck it on the car roof to take over to their place one weekend. In the middle of the LA freeway, it blew off. I wanted it back so much I considered jumping around in four lanes of traffic and getting mashed. When I eventually got myself back, I'd been gone over by fifteen major trucks.'

In a shameless hymn of love for women, for which feminists would crucify him, Hamilton told me, 'I'm very friendly with every woman I've ever been out with. I last longer than their marriages. A lot of them go away and get married for a couple of years, and then come back to me. But marriage is not on my schedule, and any woman who wants that from me can forget it.'

Is the Lady's Man a bitter chocolate cad? 'No, a cad leads a woman down the path, and then turns into a bad guy. I'm up-front with all my ladies,' said George, who takes his women at least two at a time, and sometimes by the dozen, like his vitamin pills. 'I tell them from the start "I am not going to marry you", but since women only hear what they want to hear, you have to remind them constantly. Fortunately, women's moods are constantly changing. My father taught me – "When a woman wants to cry, she's due to cry, but don't ask her why she's crying, because she probably doesn't know and it'll only add to the confusion."

'He also told me: "If a woman wants to throw things, let her, but pick out terribly expensive things for her to break, and that'll stop her right away." Most women, especially actresses, are child-like,' said the leanest roasted-brown chauvinist pig I've ever enjoyed meeting. 'A beautiful woman sees the crack in her face many years before you or I would. She doesn't really believe she's beautiful, and the loveliest women are the most insecure – that's something a lot of men never realize.

'Some women can't stand the playboy image,' confided the man who needs telephone directories where other men use little black books. 'But, actually, I'm more than just that. I know how to please a woman, and it's my joy to do it. And although I never go out with a woman I don't sexually desire, it's up to her when we get round to that. I'll take out a woman twenty-five times or more, and give her a lot of fun, and, if she still doesn't want to go to bed with me, that's her privilege. If I care for her, I'll still take her out.

'But, as for marriage, the secret of handling women is to be straightforward. Let them know what you want, and stick to it. You can never win an argument with a lady – she remembers everything you said, and nothing she said, and plays it back at you, like a tape. What you have to do is stand firm and stop her pushing too far. Women have to keep testing men to find out how far they can go. If you let them get away with it, they'll keep on pushing until there's nothing left, and then they'll hate you for it. But once they know just how far, and no further, they can go with you, women are the most adorable creatures,' smiled the Great Lothario, looking so like a glossy photograph of himself, I was tempted to ask him to autograph his own oak chest.

Hamilton, at forty-nine looking thirty-five in a good light, didn't blush to inform me that he regularly has his blood changed, as casually as putting on a fresh shirt, and that the Bottom Beautiful is injected with foetal lamb cells, so that age cannot wither him. How could even Cleopatra herself compete with that lot, at fifty-six?

In fact, I doubt that Liz Taylor, who, at any size, could push down the Walls of Jericho by blinking if she set her heart on an eighth husband, was seriously trying for George. I couldn't see him or, even if she married him for social convenience, mega-rich Malcolm Forbes, as Taylor's last Mark Antony.

Antony died with Burton. I'd been warned by her publishers not to resurrect him in conversation: 'It upsets her terribly.' Taylor herself, with a lump in her throat the size of Burton's thirty-five-carat Krupp diamond, still weighing down her wedding finger, warned me off at the start with: 'I can't read about Richard, I can't watch his films, I can't speak about him without being overcome with emotion.' She suddenly added, 'God, how we had our ups and downs, but we had more fun fighting than other people have making love,' and, choking, bolted back into the gold-tapped bathroom with, 'Forgive me, I have to blow my nose.'

She spoke freely and warmly of her marriages. Apart from her first husband, Nicky Hilton (1950–52), the billionaire son of the hotel chain who began drinking and abusing her on their honeymoon, she made all her husbands sound like the Magnificent Seven.

Michael Wilding (1952–57) was the 'great, perfect gentleman'. Of Mike Todd (1957–58), killed in the plane crash which nearly broke her spirit, she said, 'We were only married for eighteen months, but into that glorious high we packed a lifetime.' Eddie Fisher wasn't much mentioned, but never maligned. Then came Forever Burton (1964–74 and 1975) and John Warner (1976–82) who was, unwittingly, the last straw in her piling on and 'pigging out' to thirteen-and-a-half stones.

'As a senator's wife, I'd nothing to do but stay out of his way and eat chocolate fudge,' she sighed. It was Mrs Warner who dubbed herself 'the Great White Whale, pigging out in hog's heaven'. Now she told me, snorting, that, when the senator recently met the reborn Taylor, he complained, 'I liked you better fat.'

'God, after all that struggle to diet, I could have smacked him. I think he was kidding. I hope so, because he's one of my best friends,' she said. I must have looked cynical. 'Of course I care about John's future, his career, and his happiness,' she said, deadly serious. 'I don't understand couples who get divorced and then dislike each other. If you've been involved in someone's life for all those years, how can you just dismiss that? Of course love can fade, but if a man has the qualities that made you love him in the first place, how can it fade into anything but liking?'

I asked her if all her memories were sweet? And what did the now mateless Elizabeth Taylor dream of as she lay, often alone, in her Queen of Egypt-size double bed? 'My life is a swirl, a kaleidoscope of wonderful thoughts about the men I loved,' she told me. 'A single scent, a snatch of music, or just looking into the eyes of a cat which remind me of the jungle bring back my wonderful, packed life.

'How many women find two men like Mike Todd and Richard Burton? I am one lucky lady,' said the physically luckless seductress, dogged by ill health, and near death several times – 'My death from pneumonia was actually announced here in London – the best notices I ever got,' she grinned.

We couldn't know that, within weeks of my interview, her luck, and her will power, would once again run out. And that she would bury her resurrection under regained layers of fat, and blot every line of the book which had given so much hope to so many women. Looking back, the only clue was her reluctant terror of talking about 'my bloody boring back'. I couldn't resist asking if the problem was due to 'the strain of eight marriages, two of them to Burton'? or was it the child-hood fall from a horse filming *National Velvet*? 'That, and going gung-ho at ballet as a kid.' Then she added, ominously, 'If I don't get something done about it, it could get worse.' How bad? 'Look, let's just say I pray I won't spend my old age in a wheelchair, but for God's sake don't let's talk about it,' she snapped, just as she had later lashed out at the photographers who wanted to snap her in a wheelchair at Heathrow.

I'd been with her for two hours without risking the dreaded name of Sally Burton. The *Express* was disastrously losing its 'WAR OF THE WIDOWS!!!' in which I hadn't fired a single shot. When, in desperation, I took aim, Taylor jumped as if at a rifle crack. 'I won't talk about Sally, I can't speak about my feelings for Richard, it's too soon – hey, let's not get into that,' she made another dash at her eyes and the bathroom.

'THE WAR OF THE WIDOWS!!!' was going to be a very brief skirmish in print. I'd nothing to go on but my summing up of the private bloody battle between the two Mrs Burtons, and my eye witness report: 'Elizabeth Taylor's tragedy is that her Antony didn't die in his Cleopatra's arms, as we, the Burtons' untiring audience, wanted it to end. He died in the bed of Sally, twenty-two years his junior, and for thirteen months his fourth wife.'

Taylor returned from the bathroom, looking almost as drained as I now felt. She squeezed my arm: 'Tell me about you, I was so sorry to hear about.... It's every woman's greatest dread, isn't it? We all fear it. How do you learn to live with that?' Not easily, I grinned, and I've only been at it eight weeks.

She was swivelling the postage stamp Krupp on her stubby little white wedding finger. Other diamonds merely cut through glass, the Krupp is a million dollar window pane in itself. 'Isn't it vulgar?' she hooted happily. 'That's just what Princess Margaret said to me at a party – she grabbed my hand and said, "That's the most vulgar ring I've seen in my life." I asked her if she'd like to try it on – she was thrilled.'

Taylor paused, her violet eyes checking me out. Suddenly she plunged in with, 'I've always wanted to meet you, Richard often spoke about you.' I was as stunned as I've been in my professional life. Don't flatter me that my fallen girlhood hero actually remembered our single brief encounter? 'Everything, if he hadn't, how would I know all about it? He loved what you wrote about him as an actor, and not as a movie star. He used to read your stuff out loud to me, and he always said I ought to do an interview if we could fix it up.'

If we could fix it! This, from the woman of whom one frustrated, unofficial 'biographer' – Brenda Maddox, who wrote *Who's Afraid of Elizabeth Taylor?* without even meeting her subject – was reduced to excusing herself with 'Taylor hates interviews. While he lived, it was probably easier to get to Mao Tse-tung.' Admittedly the *Express* had paid £100,000 for her book, but it alone was worth that, and we'd honestly feared she would still give us the slip at the last second, or insist on being interviewed by one of a small handful of toothless, sycophantic journalists she periodically allows in to see her, knowing they will sing only a carefully rehearsed and edited hymn of praise.

So I had Burton to thank, I hoped in heaven, for giving me the big sell. 'You saw him as a young man on the stage. God, I'd have loved to have seen that! Tell me, describe it, what was he really like?' she urged me.

Inadequately, but with remembered teenage passion, I tried to bring alive for her the Boar's Head Tavern scene from Stratford's *Henry IV*, in which Prince Hal denounces his old boozing partner and mentor, Falstaff, with the audience-stunning line, 'That villainous, abominable misleader of youth, Falstaff, that old white-bearded Satan.'

'Picture the scene in the rowdy tavern,' I prompted her. 'All of them drunk and yelling, all the hangers-on, badly shaken by the Prince's words to Falstaff, but still sure they can handle the king's daft young son, and have him back in their pockets. He – Richard – was standing on a table above it all, alone. He stopped dancing, he stopped drinking, he seemed to stop breathing, he just stood there, looking down at them.

'Anthony Quayle, as Falstaff, couldn't believe what he saw in Richard's face. He started blustering, running round the table, shouting, "No, my good lord, banish Peto, banish Bardolph, banish Poins: but for sweet Jack Falstaff, kind Jack Falstaff, true Jack Falstaff, valiant Jack Falstaff, and therefore more valiant, being as he is old Jack Falstaff, banish not him thy Harry's company; banish not him thy Harry's company" – then Falstaff's last desperate throw – "banish plump Jack, and banish all the world. . . ."

'Richard hadn't moved. He still stood in the middle of the mob, like a statue of himself. Then, without even stirring a hair, he grew, he totally changed, he turned into Henry V at Agincourt, right there on the table. Very slowly – and he was young then, slim and bright-blue-eyed – he stretched out his hand and turned to point at Falstaff.

'Everyone on the stage was dead silent. So was the audience – you could have heard a feather drop, and knocked us down with it. Quayle, stunned and terrified, was crouching near a table leg, with "banish plump Jack . . .", still, like saliva, on his trembling lips. We all seemed frozen in time, like Burton. And then that fantastic Welsh voice whispered, right up to the back row of the gallery. . . ."I do. I will."'

My calling up of Burton's great ghost had been a poor wraith, but we both felt it. I was faced with another unforgettable scene – Elizabeth Taylor and I, side by side on a Dorchester sofa, staring at each other like two excited seventeen-year-olds. Ageing back to fifty-six as she poured out, with genuine anguish, 'If only I could have done for Richard what I did for myself! If only we could have done it together! I tried. When it didn't work, I divorced him for one reason. I hoped it would make him stop drinking,' she said of their first, tempestuous ten-year marriage, with its oceans of passion and endless seas of booze.

'I married him the second time because I didn't give a damn if he stopped drinking. I just wanted to be married to him,' she sighed of their second, moon-mad marriage in a Botswanian village, which ended almost as soon as the honeymoon. 'But maybe now, if he'd lived, I could have saved him. He was so proud of me after I'd been to the clinic and beaten the booze. And he was so curious about it. I honestly think he was seriously interested in looking into it, and trying to save himself. That was two months before he died.'

I honestly think his Cleopatra was, and probably still is, living out an impossible dream of a reformed, subdued, dried-out, sixty-five-year-old Antony, pottering through his coffee evenings with AA. She could never have lived with him. Better to live in hope, as she told me and TV host, Michael Aspel, that 'Richard and I will be together again one day.'

My lifelong heroine and I had shared something fine that afternoon. I'd had the lioness's share of a close look at the woman inside the blazing stardom. All I could swap her was half my 2s. 6d. seat at Burton's boyish performance, but she valued it in diamonds. As I shall always cherish her crushing honesty in stripping down the unreachable star to the middle-aged woman who had struggled to survive under her heavy burden of addiction, and her load of still unshed grief. And who was to struggle, even more cruelly, all over again.

Six months after our meeting, I was one of the 90,000 in Wembley Stadium who saw Michael Jackson break down, weeping at the start of his sensational rock concert: 'A very dear friend of mine is very, very ill. She is in unbearable pain. I would like you to bow your heads for five seconds. Her name is Elizabeth Taylor.'

At first, Taylor's entourage hotly denied that her back and will power were breaking. Within days, the stunned world knew she was back on the pills and booze, piling back three stones, in a wheelchair, and so devastated by her own back sliding, she had crawled into her darkened, now mirror-less bedroom, to hide from herself.

I remembered Gorgeous George Hamilton's words, 'The loveliest women are the most insecure, that's something a lot of men don't realize. I'll never marry again, but I'll never let a woman friend down. If she has a problem, bring it to me, because I'm good at that, I see it as my problem, and I'm there to help.'

And Hamilton was there for Taylor. The man who had shared the limelight of her Cannes come-back was as prompt to share her humiliation and pain. He wasn't ashamed to be seen with the re-fallen star, back on drink and drugs, bloated again to thirteen-and-half stones, and described by those horrified by her appearance – 'her face blotched, and her dishevelled hair white in places where it hadn't been dyed for weeks.' It was on Hamilton's genuinely good right arm, still crooked for her, that the fat, greying-haired wreck of the beauty he escorted in Cannes tottered back into the drug and alcohol clinic. By refusing to let her give up yet another fight to once again rebuild her life, Gorgeous George proved himself a kind, shining man, and put a whole new fine meaning on 'We're just good friends.'

I admire him. She has my all-time admiration, and gratitude, for what she taught me when I needed it most. At the end of that day we met, I studied my own miseries in the mirror, and reflected on what I'd learned from a Living Legend fighting to live on. We all have our weary loads. Our cracked mirrors. Our hidden terrors behind closed doors. The world is teeming with unsung Elizabeth Taylors, struggling as gallantly as Taylor herself to survive.

CHAPTER ◆ NINE

Facing the Foe

As the cancer specialist pored, enthralled, over my bosom, it was his eyes I was watching. And praying not to see that flash of recognition, or flicker of fear, before the heart-stopping, 'Look, I'm sorry to have to tell you this, but . . . .'

'Sweat like hell the night before you come to see me, everybody does,' the man had said three months ago. 'But for the rest of the time, forget it.' The dozen times a day I'd nagged her, 'Are you sure I look all right?' my mother had put the same point more sharply. 'Jean, if you're going to spend your life between check-ups scared stiff that you're going to die, what's the point of living?'

Lying half-stripped on a hospital couch, ludicrously like an ageing Josephine waiting for Napoleon, I was sweating a Niagara at my second check-up. I guessed that the initial check, a month after radiotherapy treatment ended, had been mostly a surface skin examination of my healing scars. And that, even if the damned thing was re-arming itself to attack me, it wouldn't have had time to grab hold.

By now, they should know if the enemy within was really

out, or already creeping stealthily back for another ambush. As I lay staring up at him like a beseeching trapped rabbit, the oncologist's eyes were grey glass crystals in which I couldn't read my future, or lack of it. I suppose these chaps are trained not to scream and faint. And, face it, why should he? I'm sure the man cares, and wants me to live, but, if my number's up, I am only a listed number, and it is only the end of his hard working day, not his world. He's not going to crack up in tears and rush, demented, round the building, sounding sirens and pulling plugs like those glamorous, sun-tanned interns in *General Hospital*.

Real life – and real, gaunt, lipstickless death – isn't like an American soap opera where the patient dies, fully made-up and radiant, as the Ryan O'Neal-type consultant walks down a mile-long corridor towards the camera, and the sobbing relatives, choking, 'Believe me, we did all we could . . .'

'That's fine, I'll see you again in two months,' my man handed me back my life as casually as my faded flowered cotton NHS gown. What would he have said if it hadn't been? 'I'd have told you straight, "something's wrong", and what we could do to put it right. I said from the start I'd never bullshit you,' he grinned, boyishly eager, now we'd got the business over and bundled it back into my bra, for a detailed first-hand re-examination of my interview with Joan Collins in that morning's *Express*.

Genuinely intrigued by my 'fascinating life', he was mod-estly unable to see himself, as I did, as the guardian and monitor of it. In his coffee break, we did a fair swap. He pumped me about Collins. I probed him on women's reaction to finding The Lump.

'There are two sorts of women – the one like you who's scared out of her wits the second she touches it, and rushes round to the doctor screaming *"Do it now!"* Women in their forties and fifties usually can't wait to get at the truth and get something done about it, thank God. There are terrible exceptions,' he said sadly. 'I had one young woman who came to me, pregnant, with a lump she must have hidden for a couple of years. Heaven knows how she'd managed to have sex with her husband without his finding out. It was a stage four by this time – a lump with surrounding lumps that had spread into her lymph glands and her body. She died. If only she'd come to us when she first found it, two years earlier, we could easily have treated her.

'The other type of woman who just can't face it, is often in her sixties and seventies. She doesn't want to know, so she deliberately ignores it, convincing herself it will go away. She literally hides the thing even from herself. The lump is getting bigger, and she must know it's eating away at her physically, but, mentally, she somehow switches off. She stubbornly refuses to see it, touch it, or believe it – she'll be all right so long as she doesn't have to know.'

When does she have to? 'When it turns into something really dramatic even she can't ignore – often a bleeding ulcer on the surface. Of course, by the time it's that dramatic, it's too late.'

Cancer is the ugliest disease. In real life, as in some fiction, can it be glamorized, even glorified by the victim's bravery? Since I first read it, in teenage, I'd been swept away by the noble, albeit fictional grandeur with which Daphne du Maurier's heroine, Rebecca, received her death sentence.

The scene is compulsive. The ravishing Rebecca, with her 'boy's slim figure and the face of a Botticelli angel', is riddled with cancer. Age not specified, but not a dazzling day over thirty-six. The doctor is stunned by the physical presence of this 'most beautiful creature I ever saw in my life', whom he's about to condemn to death.

'I remember her perfectly well,' the doctor said. 'Tall, slim, dark, very beautiful. She came to me a week before the date you mentioned. She complained of certain symptoms, and I took X-rays of her. The second visit was to find out the result of those X-rays. I remember her standing in my consulting room, holding out her hand for the photographs. "I want to know the truth," she said. "I don't want soft words or a bedside manner. If I'm for it, you can tell me right away."

'Outwardly, of course, she was a perfectly healthy woman. Rather too thin, rather pale, but that's the fashion nowadays, more's the pity. It's nothing to go on with a patient. No, the pain would increase week by week, and, in four or five months, she would have had to be kept under morphia.

'Well, she'd asked for the truth, and I let her have it. Some patients are better for it. Shirking the point does them no good. This Mrs Danvers, or Mrs de Winter rather, was not one to accept a lie. You must have known that. She stood it very well. She did not flinch. She said she had suspected it for some time. Then she paid my bill and went out. I never saw her again.'

Re-reading this, I still get delicious spine shivers. So when they told me I had cancer, why hadn't I behaved like a latter day Rebecca, poised for her Grand Exit? And does anybody, in real, terrified life?

'I knew one – a marvellous looking woman, a truly gorgeous redhead with two young children,' my specialist said. 'I think she was twenty-eight – a particularly terrible shock because breast cancer is much rarer in women under forty-five. Maybe it helped that she was a nurse, but she was as cool as a cucumber, didn't turn a hair when I told her it meant a mastectomy. She thanked me for my help, and said it was fine, she knew just what she had to face.'

I couldn't face asking if she lived or died. I'm not in Rebecca's stylish class.

'Only one in a million is,' the doctor comforted me. 'At least twenty-five per cent of the patients here in hospital, being treated for it, won't actually say the words "I've got cancer". They will say "I'm in here for a cyst". That's the way they have to play it, by disguising it. It's their way of coping, their defence. So we go along with it, and never say "cancer" either.'

Why is cancer dirtier than any four-letter word, even AIDS? 'Ordinary folk don't come across AIDS every day, so it doesn't mean much to them. They don't see it yet as the next Great

Plague which will take over from cancer as the world's big horror disease. Everyone is frightened of cancer, because everyone knows someone who's died of it, and, until five or six years ago, people thought of it as an automatic death sentence. Most people over thirty-five still do. You must have had relatives who died of it?'

My father, and an unlucky half dozen aunts, I totted up dejectedly. 'How old were they?' From seventy-two to eighty-six, I added up, brightening. 'That's just it, people do tend to forget that we all have to die at some stage, and cancer is the commonest form of death in old people. The dramatic cancer cases among the young or the famous are the ones you read about. But, in fact, most people's exposure to cancer is the elderly relative who dies of it at the end of a decent innings. We've all had an Aunt Fannie or an Uncle Fred who popped off with it. It's worth remembering that if cancer hadn't got dear old Uncle Fred, at nearly eighty, he'd have died of a heart attack a few days later.'

It's wonderfully cheering how people who live, work, eat, sleep, freely talk about and daily fight with cancer, see it not as The End in itself, but only as the Grim Reaper's nastiest weapon which it's their life's quest to destroy.

But what precisely *is* breast cancer, besides an evil seed, a hideous predator, and a cruel abomination to the 14,500 women in Britain alone who annually die of it? 'How simply do you want me to put this?' asked the oncologist. At play-school level. Draw me it in big, coloured crayons. Explain to me just what I've got, when, why, and what happens next.

He said drily that only God ultimately knows what happens next. But he didn't mind having a shot in the dark ignorance which surrounds cancer and its treatment, and at the terrible tales told mostly by old wives who've never had it.

'We all have things called "oncogenes" in our bodies,' he said. 'Normally, their function in a healthy system is to react with, and regulate, other normal cells. In people who don't get cancer, that's how it works. But in some of us, and why some of us are chosen is still being researched, these oncogenes get misplaced. They become un-organized, misbehave, go berserk. Instead of regulating the cells, they let them run wild, mount up, get out of control and increase to form masses and clusters.'

And terrifying bumps inside your nightgown in the night? 'Exactly so. These uncontrolled cells become malignant tumours. I estimated your lump at at least one, maybe even two years old, but any estimate is necessarily rough. Cancer starts with a single berserk cell which doubles, and then re-doubles, but it can take a hell of a time before the thing grows to the size of your thumbnail, and something you can actually feel. That's why we need unilateral screening, to help us catch it almost as soon as it takes root.'

Not passionately keen to know, but ever the investigative hackette, I asked him if, having had it once, I'm more likely to get breast cancer tomorrow than the next spotless, lumpless woman? 'Yes,' he said. 'You've already proved that by having it once.' I'm all for sparsity of bullshit, but couldn't this bloke find a smidge of artificial fertilizer in which I could plant my hopes?

'You know the score well enough,' he grinned. 'On paper, you've a sixty per cent chance – some put it much higher – of never seeing another thing. And a forty per cent chance of finding something we could still do a lot about if it came to it. Get on with your life, or you'll still be dithering in your boots when you come for a check-up at eighty. And when you're eighty, I'll probably have to tell you you've got cancer.'

No you won't, I beamed back. By that time they'll be zapping us with lasers in our lunch hours, like *Star Wars*.

Meantime, how do they stop the risk of my further rot? 'The biggest break-through in breast cancer is tamoxifen. We may not be able to stop oncogenes becoming malignant, but with tamoxifen we can prevent the female hormones working with them to form cancer. At its simplest, think of the female hormone as a little key that latches on to the oncogene and turns it into a cancer cell. What tamoxifen does is sit in the lock and block the cancer.'

Tamoxifen may be hailed as a modern miracle, all done with two aspirin-size tablets a day for life, and no side effects, but how sure was he, I probed shrewdly, about the side effects? The daily drug was tampering with my excitable female hormones. How would I know if, as he said, it was merely holding the fort against them, or secretly slaughtering them and turning me into Sappho? What if my voice plunged three octaves and I grew a beard?

And tamoxifen does have side effects – I was expansive proof. In the three months I'd been taking the little life-savers, I'd put on half a stone. Doubling my size might be a small price for enlarging my life span, but was there a way out of what looked like ballooning into a marquee?

'You will not grow a beard, or hairs on your chest, and what have you been eating that you didn't before your lumpectomy?' he demanded sternly. Everything, I admitted miserably. Chips, chocolates, ice cream, crisps, even an Easter egg at 4 a.m. on Christmas Day.

For three months I'd crammed in, with a shovel, stuff I hadn't touched with tongs in years. I was nightly creeping downstairs to raid Gresby's sweet cupboard, and daily re-filling it in fear of a flying visit from school. I was a physical pig with the cunning of a rat. 'I got this fixation that people with cancer get thin and gaunt,' I said. Even to me it sounded like a gross excuse.

'People with terminal cancer do,' he said severely. 'People who've had a primary operation who could stuff themselves for another twenty-five years, just get fat.'

I loved the man so much for these nourishing words, I could have eaten him alive, without salt.

I knew it was time, now that I had some – to assess my new situation. And to weigh up and measure what was left of me. At five-foot-seven-and-a-half-inches, I had been a passable ten stones four, and a good size 36C up top. I was now a depressing eleven stones, most of it on the backside I'd been forced to sit and lie on for weeks, and 36C right cup, 34B left cup not filled to the brim. 'I think you've reached about the best balance you can hope for,' the oncologist mused, his eye trained on my angles like a theodolite.

I look like a seesaw, I snapped. 'You look fine, as good as

new with a bra on,' he said, promising that the slightly scaly artificial 'suntan' of radiotherapy would eventually iron out and fade. 'That scar's a bit lumpy, though,' he admitted.

I was no lovely sight. My tired face was paper white for lack of fresh air, my straw-straight hair hung down like yellowing raffia. But there I was. Not all I used to be, but enough to rebuild my life on, and salvage my career.

After all, I'd been born overweight. And born nearly blind, with eyesight you wouldn't wish on a cross-eyed pup. I'd still clawed and scrambled my way to become Fleet Street's First Bitch, and the highest paid woman journalist in Britain. I'd overcome bigger mountains than an eroded and rocky boob in my time. At fifty-six, and after cancer, I hadn't all the time in my badly shaken world to start again at the beginning. But, give me some time, and I'd prove that it wasn't the end.

That night, I wrote the first ten, nervous pages of this book. And prayed for the time, and strength, to finish it, and know that I wasn't yet finished.

CHAPTER ◆ TEN

The Ugly Cub

*O*n the bleak Friday 13 November when I weighed into the world at 9lb 10oz, my narrow-hipped, seven-and-a-half-stone mother nearly died. So did my father when they told him it was a girl. My sixteen-stone sire was not only built like Henry VIII, he had the same views on progeny – I'd been referred to as Peter for months.

One look at me, swears my mother, and Pa's entire outlook on the world shifted. Boys were just babies, girls were miracles of nature. What did it matter, he comforted mother, that the doctor had advised against the risk of her having more children? His big, beautiful, bouncing blonde baby, who already looked like Boadicea, would take over his firm, rule his life, and eventually govern the nation. (Pa hadn't reckoned on a Grantham grocer's six-year-old daughter, seventy-three miles away on the opposite side of the Humber, called Margaret Hilda Roberts.)

To conquer the world, you have to be able to see it clearly. At eight months, I had an indoor swing suspended above the bath. Pitching to and fro in the nude, I must have looked like an innocent version of that steamy scene in *The Stud* where

Joan Collins shuttles naked across a swimming pool in a hanging basket of flowers. It was on the upswing, as I rushed towards her, gurgling like the bath taps, that my mother noticed my right eye vanish into the corner. It was more than a slight squint. My by-now brown owl-like eye seemed hell bent on finding out what went on behind my nose.

While my perceptive mother topped up the bath with anxious tears, Father stubbornly refused to see a flaw in the flesh of his flesh. For a week, he dashed home early from his office to swing me seasick over the bath, glaring at me, storming 'Her eye does *not* move!' On the Friday night, my right eye dived behind my nose, while my left glowered at Pa like a lop-sided Cyclops.

Next morning, Hull's leading eye specialist broke it to my heartbroken parents that I was acutely long-sighted and astigmatic, and couldn't even see them except through a permanent fuzz. Long-sighted people spend their lives explaining it doesn't mean you're a human hawk who can spot a pin a mile off, but that the eyeball is so short the image overshoots the retina at the back of it. Unless we shorten our focal length by squinting we live in a blurred world, like the moon with a ring round it.

If I wasn't to end up as swivel-eyed as Quasimodo, I must be fitted immediately with doll-size gold wire specs. But how do you persuade an eight-month-old baby that wearing glasses is more fun than building blocks? The far-sighted optician who made my 5p-size lenses summoned his entire staff to his office: 'I want everyone in glasses, whether you need them or not.' I was surrounded by intriguing, shining people bending over me, slipping their marvellous moon eyes on and off. Offered my own mini-pair, I grabbed for the magic windows and rammed them on.

Convinced that, if I could take them off again, I'd swallow them within twenty-four hours, the optician fixed them on my button nose with an elastic band round my head. My mother cried all the way home, pushing what now looked like a forlorn barn owl sitting up in its pram.

The best the optician could offer my mother and her bottle-eyed baby was, 'At fourteen, she'll be able to take her glasses off and walk around, go to dances without them. She'll even be able to "accommodate" – that is tighten the eyeball by pulling a muscle without squinting – for a few seconds, long enough to read a phone number or a shop price tag. She'll never read properly, or see a cinema or theatre without them, of course. At thirty-five, the accommodating muscle will begin to wear out – she'll start having trouble with three, five and eight in the phone book. After that, I'm afraid it'll just get hazier. By forty-five, she'll be so sick of walking under buses, she'll be glad to get back into glasses.'

At eight months, you are never going to be fourteen. At fourteen, you're certainly never going to see a decrepit, dim-sighted forty-five. Both came. I saw, more or less. I finally conquered with contact lenses. But in the meantime I was to see much misery, mostly of my own making.

As a toddler I was Goldilocked, with such a striking resemblance to 'Bubbles' that a talent scout from a famous rusk firm who spotted me on the beach at Skegness, offered my mother a fortune, and me instant fame, chuckling on a rusk packet. Because their brand made me throw up, my honest Yorkshire mother didn't send in my photograph.

By late kindergarten, my Goldilocks had already turned boringly brown as the Three Bears. But like all little thirties girls, I fantasized myself as a floating-haired fairy princess, and turned into a shrieking demon, at seven, when my mother tried to cut it off. Since, in my day, school teachers lopped off your head, never mind your hair, if it didn't hygieni-cally clear your blouse collar, I was forced to weave my frustrated fantasies, from 8 a.m.–4 p.m., into a pair of mousey plaits.

At the age of eight, with stout legs, massive rear, and horn-rimmed specs, I looked like a blinkered carthorse. In that pre-pop era, girls were just spot-prone little girls, not mini Madonnas. What God gave you was it, at least until sweet or sour sixteen, when you could start re-jigging nature with paint, powder and your first heady perm. Anorexia was publicly unheard of. Dieting under the age of eighteen, virtually unknown. If you were a fat kid, you were lumped with it.

And fat was fun, at least until eighteen months. Big, bruising, nappy-splitting babies were prized, and won silver cups at baby shows. If you still smashed scales in teenage, aunts beamed that you were 'bonny', you conned yourself you were 'big-boned', and only your cruel-tongued schoolmates put you into perspective as 'Bessie Bunter', or in my bespectacled case, 'Four-Eyed Fatima'. Nothing strips your excuse to yourself that 'it's only puppy fat' like the fangs of the svelte, seven-stone bitch in the next desk.

Little as I remember of World War II, I do recall the dreadful day Hull sent up its first barrage balloons – huge winged rubber melons in the sky – to protect us from enemy aircraft. Even before milk break, my mirthfully exploding schoolmates had labelled me the Big Barrage. As these daily taunts grew massive in my mind, I hid from my tormentors in the fridge. Comfort eating, of course, only enlarged the vicious circle of my too-tight box-pleated gym-slip. I detested those pleats. On thin girls the boxes stayed knife-edged, and close-packed, side by side. On me they split open like damp cardboard cartons, spilling my hefty hips.

It was our wartime move to the solitary Yorkshire moors which gave me, if not gossamer wings, at least the freedom to live like the fantastic, glamorous creature struggling inside my podgy little person. On the daisy-chained lawns of Westerdale Hall, our twin-turreted enchanted castle, I could dance, unseen, by moonlight. Shrink to the size of a sylph. Live happily ever after in the mists of imagination behind my hideous gold wire specs.

I rode well, and had to, in winter, hacking through the snowdrifts to the station to travel to school. But now, in my magic-making mind, I was no longer a big-bummed Thelwell caricature of a child on a barrel-shaped pony. I was the Wicked Lady, thundering over the moors with a mane of flying jet black hair to match my snorting stallion. In summer, having no-one to play tennis with but a stable door, I would

Wimbledon away for hours, banging out romantic stories in which I was the heart-stopping heroine.

In my golden-hazy daydreams I was 'Yvonne', and for years nagged my parents to change my name in conversation, if not by deed poll. Yvonne was slender as my racket handle, with spot-on focussed eyes as big as lily ponds, and ebony heel-length hair. She always wore virgin white, or knowing scarlet, and, on really imaginative days, was swept off her size two feet (mine were already size eight) by my six-foot-four-inch hero who draped her feather-light body over his muscle-bound arm.

While mentally knocking out this amateur Mills and Boon, I was incidentally, but unerringly, clouting the third plank from the left on the stable door. By summer's end, I could beat that plank to pulp, forehand, backhand, smash and volley, 6–0, 6–0. The stable door's tireless coaching paid off. Bouncing boobed and bottomed as I was, and heavy on my feet, my bespectacled eye for a ball was a killer. I was a smash at the game. I won my first, thrilling respect from my flattened peers when I played and won for the school. Later I scored heftily at London University, and, had I made club and county tennis my life's work, could probably have reached at least the outside courts at Wimbledon.

I still shift a nifty ball. When Gresby, at ten, laconically rang from prep school, to say they were short for the Mothers' Match, so he'd put me down ('You *can* play, can't you?') I rooted out my dear old Slazenger and my yellowing Ted Tinling frilly knickers and started knocking hell out of our garage door. On Match Day I whizzed through the first round, slammed through the second, and, partnered by a mother who unfairly blinded our schoolboy opponents by playing with shocking pink balls to match her socks, won the day.

Gresby, who had watched this performance with eyes so bulgingly round you could have used them as spare balls, was so silent over our restaurant dinner I could hear my already stiffening limbs creaking every time I tried, agonized, to move. 'You are pleased with me, aren't you?' I volleyed anxiously.

'Mum, you just beat the best boy in the school, wrecked his

sports day, and made a complete dork of me!' Gresby lobbed back. 'I told him to hit everything straight at you, because you'd be bound to be rotten and hit nothing back. How the hell did I know you were going to play like Navratilova?'

With children, who can win? If only Gresby had known what a loser I was at his age. Though not academically. For all my batty eyesight, I was born with a photographic memory like a Nikon on motor drive. You name it, I'd snap it straight back at you, verbatim. Thus, passing the 11-plus from my very mixed little village school to the great Yorkshire grammar, Whitby County School, was as easy as spilling all my pent-up learning-by-heart from the fountain pen which scribbled me a County Major Award and a State Scholarship. Both financially useless, since Pa was too rich to pass the means test.

Writing nine straight grade ones at O level was just as simple, if you knew how. And I knew how, though not necessarily why. Physics and chemistry, not one experiment of which I could handle, would have been a closed book if I hadn't worked out that, at relatively humble O-level, all you need is to deliver the goods. If it had put in the tedious time and endless slog that I did, Long John Silver's parrot could have filled in my exam papers.

Except, of course, in maths, where you have to actually do something, on the day, with what you know. I could do 0–10 every time. I once achieved a school record of nil per cent for geometry. Of the thirty-two in our maths class, I was unerringly thirty-first. The girl who never failed to hit rock bottom was called Troy Young, and her name, and a graph of her beloved, puzzled face, are forever traced on my heart. After yards of extra coaching, I scratched a discreditable maths O by a whisker.

From A-levels through university, it was plain, swift sailing in the chosen specialist subjects I relished. My Bedford College tutors marked me down for a guaranteed first class degree – couldn't miss. For the five days of Finals, I just sat there, writing my ticket. Then, on the last question of the last paper of the last exam, I ripped it up. I couldn't understand the obligatory question on Restoration drama. Since my mind has mercifully buried the suicide of my brilliant academic future, I can't now remember the fatal question.

I sweatingly remember reading it one way, then re-reading it another, as the white-faced exam room clock ate up the ever dwindling sixty minutes I had left to make or break a First. With ten minutes left, the light broke like a switched-on arc lamp. I could see it clearly, knew it all, but hadn't the time left even to scrawl it down. I outlined what I would have written, and missed a First by two marks. They were the best two marks I didn't make in my life. With a First to back up the MA I went on to get, Bedford would have nailed me to an English teacher's desk, and I'd probably now be head-mistress of Saint Somewhere.

As a plain, fat, determinedly extrovert, but secretly intro-verted eleven-year-old in my new grammar school uniform – box pleats again, dammit! – my lessons in Life were more painfully learned than maths. Since my father, mother and I were lovingly close-knit – The Three Musketeers, Pa called us – my home life was warmly secure. The door of a carriage on the 8.20 from Castleton to Whitby was the first to be slammed in my face.

We travelled to the County School at wind-lashed, coastal Whitby, by steam train. (Nearly forty years later, when my small son squealed for a puff-puff on the North Yorkshire Moorland Railway, still running for entranced tourists, I was winded to find myself back in my dear old school carriage. I knew it from the scuff marks we made, hanging upside down by our shoes from the mahogany-and-string parcel racks.)

The coveted carriage was 'bagged' by a real life fairy princess of a fourteen-year-old beauty called . . . ah well, perhaps not, time's supposed to heal all, and I'm about to kick her in her by now probably false teeth. But, God, back then she was physically everything I ached to be. She had long, flip-up eyelashes, and, when she loosed it from school-rule ribbons, long, flip-under hair. The wartime hair-do was the 'pageboy', terribly difficult to do unless you had thick, smooth locks which turned inwards at the bottom like Richard III's.

Her pageboy was a black satin sheet. I still had stringy plaits.

I yearned to be a member of her smart set, a small corner of her most glamorous carriage on the train in which, since the school was mixed, there were boys. Long-limbed fifth form boys, with massive muscular chests probably size 38 at most, but my envious specs enlarged them. Cherished, all right spoilt, as I was as an only child, I thought all I had to do to join was ask. She sneered at me. So did her two slim, alluring classmates who shared the boys in her carriage. They poked fun at my jealously staring 'four eyes', and gaping box pleats. As a taunting team, the three of them could have stood in for Macbeth's witches.

More terrifyingly, they kept threatening me with a 'curse' which was about to smite me down like the Lady of Shalott. My bloody-minded tormentors had discovered I didn't know about menstruation. At that time, close-lipped middle-class mothers never quite knew how to put it delicately and, in my case, mother was wretchedly staving off telling me about the monthly hell I would have to go through, cycling and horse-riding to the station. One day I slammed down my foot and my satchel. What was this Aeschylean curse those girls had laid on me? When my crimson-cheeked mother explained, I could have killed her for letting me live in terror of a Red Death from my schoolmates, compared with which the uncomfortable monthly cycle across the moors proved to be nothing.

I admitted to mother that life was a bitch aged fourteen in another train carriage. 'I see, let me think about it,' she said. The next time my father came home on leave from the Army, he took me fishing. 'Why don't you start your own carriage?' he said, out of the clear blue summer sky, as we sat shoulder to shoulder, and heart to heart on the river bank.

Oh my dear father, how many times, in the next twenty-five years, did you start an almost daily phone call or letter with, 'It's just an idea for you, but why don't you . . .?' You saw no bounds to my ability, no limits to my skies. We two were a single mighty force, always driving towards what you never doubted would be my success. I still take strength from your fading, Victorian copperplate letters – the advice, praise, unfailing encouragement, pinned to a £1 note. Your final, feebly penned note, 'Thank you for a wonderful weekend, in fact thank you for everything.' The Batman and Robin birthday card: 'It's you and me against the world – I'd say the odds were about even!' And the last, crumpled leaf from your daily motto desk calendar: 'The past should be used as a springboard, not as a sofa.'

I remember every last word, that weekend before you died. 'You belong to a new era of women, I always knew it would come one day. In the next few years, the world will open up to women as never before, and that world is your oyster, you can do anything with it. Take care of your mother, but never fear that she'll fall to pieces on her own, she won't. Listen to her, as you've always listened to me. I know you think she's just the homemaker who's never had a proper job, or written a cheque. But where do you think I got my strength which you admire so much? The same place you'll get your strength when I'm gone. Never underestimate your mother, because, I promise you, she'll amaze you.'

She has, since the day of my father's funeral, when one of the tactless Lincolnshire aunts whacked the last nail in the coffin with, 'What a tragedy Horace never had a son to carry on his name.'

'A son! What did 'Race need with a son?' my string-thin mother grew to my father's size, and rounded on her. 'What son could have given him more joy, been closer to him, worked harder to make him proud? Never let me hear any of you say that again. And never let me hear you say it, and don't even think it,' she whipped round on me. 'Your father never wanted any child but the one he got – you, and only *you*.'

Beloved Father, if ever I wrote my autobiography, I'd planned to write it for you. Now all the water has run by the river bank where we talked away our golden summers, and there are no words to match the best friend and father you were, and are, to me. After twenty years, never a day of my life goes by without you. So I've dedicated the book you always knew I'd write one day to the name you would be proudest to see on the fly leaf. To your truly amazing wife.

The material for my railway carriage wasn't richly promising stuff. We were remnants, really, the kids established carriages didn't want. There was my elephantine, mousy-plaited self; an equally plain classmate with a chest flatter than the Adam's apple of the one lost, pencil-thin boy we persuaded to join us; and a truly beautiful but totally dumb blonde, who would have been our carriage's star turn could she have coupled two words together.

But we were creative. We invented the infamous parcel rack somersault – hands apart, shin up the plush seat-back between the pock-marked pictures of Whitby Abbey, turn over and hang by your heels like a navy blue flannel bat. Other carriages grabbed on to this, and to our ploy for keeping out joy-killing adult passengers by steaming up our carriage windows with plague-like coughs and sneezes until the train pulled out.

Gradually, even the toffiest noses in the school began to press against our misted-up windows to see what was going on that they hadn't thought of. And we were physically changing – miraculously, stupendously – overnight; and almost between stations. Flat Chest developed tennis balls under her straining gymslip. Adam's Apple suddenly seemed to have swallowed one as he filled out. Dumb Blonde, past puberty, didn't need to breathe a word – she'd only to breathe in to crash the entire train.

And my time had come. I was still heavyweight, but my sands had shifted, and resettled into a 42–28–43 hourglass. I was a thirteen-year-old Lady Chatterley, in love with our gardener's seventeen-year-old son, who would have moved the earth for me with his bare hands. The earthy lad, whose father tilled for mine, had a job in a moorland pottery works just off my school route, and our cycle paths crossed. Sun, rain, hail and snow, we would pedal home, side by palpitating side, our hands – wet and slippery with budding sex and the appalling weather – clasped under our daffodil yellow oilskin bicycle capes. One late afternoon, in Westerdale's quietest spot, behind the graveyard wall, we explored our blossoming bodies. It was too damply chill to do anything, and, although my biology ran to it, I knew my parents would fling fits if we conducted a practical experiment.

Oh, but it was ignorant, innocent love among the heather that summer I was lucky thirteen. In my admirer's eyes I was the only slender-hocked filly in the show. To hell, now, with the girl with the flip-up eyelashes and flip-under hair. Heathcliff was mine.

The war's end ended my first great romance, chaste as the snow my virgin lover and I had chilblained through in winter, but as deep. I equated Hull, to which we were returning, with Hell. 'I'll oft think of thee,' he said in his purple moorland dialect, as we sat, wet-eyed on the packed wooden crates. 'I'll never forget you,' I cried from a broken teenage heart.

Four decades later, on a sentimental journey to show Gresby my heathery roots, I stopped at a moorland garage. It was the owner's hands, so often held in mine, I noticed before his still deep purple voice. 'By God, lass,' he said, respectfully running a wash leather over the leaping silver Jaguar on my bonnet, 'if I'd married thee, we might have been riding round in this car.'

'If I'd married thee, we wouldn't, but we'd have had this view from your window,' I said, gazing over the distant rounded hills and secret hollows in which we had pledged our deathless love.

I wasn't so bucked to hear from *her* of the sensational eye lashes, after I'd appeared on *Wogan*. 'You won't remember me,' her letter gushed (oh, come on, dear, you are as indelibly inked on me as the name tag on my old school blouse!) 'but I often think of you, and the wonderful times we had together at school.' Vengeance may be the Lord's, but who could resist smiting the tormentor who had slammed the door in my plain, spotty, spectacled face? Then I read on, and on, about her dreary semi-detached existence, several children, but more problems, and her pitiful excitement at touching the fringe of what must be my 'glamorous and exciting' life. She had no more perception, at fifty-four, than she had at fourteen. I shelved her letter at the bottom of the readers' pile, and eventually sent a note to say how much I valued our schoolgirl friendship.

Hull, blasted by Hitler to one massive, bomb site car park, was Hell. But life, at fourteen, was Paradise, after a visit to the eye specialist who ordered me to get 'em off – even though the prognosis, at fourteen, was as gloomy as at eight months. Who can convince Cinderella that, at midnight, her white horses will change back into mice? I blundered blissfully down the eye specialist's stairs into my Golden Age. My out-of-focus face was now a mezzotint, half seen in the mirror through a romantic haze. I never touched the fringe of beauty, or even made it half way to pretty. But nip-waisted, lush-bosomed, and swelling-hipped, with near-blind eyes like ripe figs, I had sex appeal by the barrel.

The best autobiographies surge with emotional traumas. Traumatically, I'm a let-down. Apart from one potentially crippling set-back from a married man who jilted me from a great height, at twenty-four, my early sex life was like my tennis – slam, bam, standard strokes.

I did, at twelve, escape rape by a middle-aged farmer who, one winter's afternoon in his barn, began, slobbering, to climb the ladder to where I was a sitting pigeon in his hay loft. Innocence, and almost complete sexual ignorance, was my breastplate. I grabbed a pitchfork, stood at the ladder top like Britannia, and threatened to trumpet to the village that Farmer X was a wicked, dirty old man.

If I seem to be dismissing a brutal subject too lightly, I am only recording the way thousands of innocent British children were in the war. We were battered by Hitler's bombs, and starved of rationed Mars bars, but our lives were almost totally sheltered from sexual violence. Those were the long-gone days when a schoolgirl could ride the same daily route over a misty moor, with no risk of ending up molested and mutilated in a ditch. We *were* the Ovaltinies. Sexual atrocities were virtually unheard of. Lolita was unborn. The only teenager we knew who'd got herself into deadly trouble was Romeo's Juliet, and she was too removed from real, hockey-playing life to be a fourteen-year-old role model.

My adoration of my father was no Electra complex – I never fancied a man remotely like him, but tended to hunt down rather stricken-looking Percy Bysshe Shelleys. The great love of my school life was called Michael, who looked to my eyes like the Archangel in a bottle green blazer. My father's description of him as 'a long thin yard of pump water' didn't damp my ardour.

My passionate necking with Michael went as far as I dared. Everything was thoroughly removed and gone into except the final, frail veil of virginity. In my dinosaurean day, you went up to university with your father's admonition, 'No gambling or bridge debts, and no sex before marriage,' ringing in your ears.

To keep Michael on his toes, I incidentally kicked around a bit with the huge-thighed school football captain, and deliberately scored at least one date with all seven members of the sixth form so that I could list the entire team in my diary. Then I lost an asset more precious to me than my virginity, or at the time, my life. I lost my front tooth.

One milk break, I was accidentally smacked in the mouth by an upflung desk lid. Michael straddled me for twenty minutes, gallantly holding in the tooth, now swinging like a cat flap. It stayed in, but, within a week, had discoloured to a bruised-looking brown. I had it capped, but, only weeks later, developed an abscess in the roots. The dentist broke it to me that the whole lot, root and cap, would have to come out.

My life was shattered, finished at seventeen. I was inadequate, maimed, less than all-woman. Nothing could fill the gap. Since those were the days when they didn't instantly fit your false tooth, I stayed home and crawled into a hole to hide the hole in my face from the world. Michael flew round to comfort me, but was lisped at, from behind my barred bedroom door, 'Donth you dare to tryth to come in or I'll jumpth out of the window.' He pressed himself against my sobbing, ruined body. 'I wasn't going to tell you this until I had to, but look here,' he said.

Then, like a magician, he removed both his gleaming white Archangelic front teeth. 'I had them knocked out by an oar at twelve,' he said. My Dartford tunnel was nothing compared with his Mersey. Knowing what pride it had cost him to restore mine, I sprang at him, and we clung together – two teenage vampires locked, almost literally, in a necessarily very sloppy kiss.

When I went up to London University, and Michael to Trinity College, Dublin, our romance slowly foundered in the Irish sea. The distance was too great, and the vacations too short. Our eventual parting of the ways was mutually agreed, but my memories are still fond.

All my packed girlhood memories are fond. I am, always have been, and trust I shall be to my last breath, extremely keen on men. I have never burned a bra, and, until my operation forced me temporarily into white cotton, my bras were plunging black lace.

I'm often asked, in the hope that I'll fire one for feminism, about my attitude to Women's Lib. I can only applaud the climate it has created for increased opportunities and pay, but in fact I detest red-hot, militant feminists. I've no time for hairy arm-pitted females, with unshaven legs, whose idea of equality is kicking men in the groin.

I'm grateful that my father's prediction, 'The world will open up for women as never before', has come true in the twenty years since his death. But as one who's done more than most to open it up in my own profession, I've never found any need to be deliberately bloody-minded to men, to attempt to shove male colleagues into Fleet Street's gutters, or, like some much lesser women journalists than myself, to make a scratching, bitching fool of myself trying to tear down the door of the men only bar in El Vino's.

I most succinctly summed up my views on frustrated, over-militant feminism, in a recent message in my column to the great, self-styled liberator, Germaine Greer:

I assume that intensely dreary woman, Germaine Greer, realizes she speaks for herself by dismissing all flaccid-flanked British men as 'homosexual'. Since she's been talking by herself, about herself, and in the main to herself for the past twenty years, I am weary of this middle-aged, unmarried, childless, self-appointed sexpert telling me all about men. I'm not convinced Ms Greer knows all about men, or even the half of it.

Prime beefy example of Australian womanhood as she is, Ms Greer, at fifty-three, is no Antipodean Joan Collins. For spectacular looks, Dame Edna Everage beats her hollow. We have only Ms Greer's word – thousands of them – that she has sampled a liquorice assortment of dozens of lovers of all races, colours and creeds which qualifies her to issue world wide sex ratings. She rates Brits and Aussies as gay, the French vain, Americans stiff – but only with fear of women – and Arabs useless at night. Only the Italian stallion, of which we're invited to believe old Germaine has had whinnying herds, escapes her tongue lash.

Exactly what has Ms Greer achieved, which justifies her jumping on men's libidos like an ageing kangaroo? She was married at thirty-three, for three weeks. Thwarted in her frustrated forties by what she and all her militant kind call, 'the twentieth century tragedy – by the time I realized I wanted children it was too late'.

Has it ever struck her that ordinary women have children and ideas at the same time? Her fame as a rabid feminist rests on two books. *The Female Eunuch*, the feminists' Bible, is now eighteen years old. In *Sex and Destiny*, published four years ago, by fruitlessly glorifying 'wrongly degenerated motherhood', she contradicts everything she was chump enough to write in the first place.

I have never seen, heard, or read Ms Greer apparently happily relaxed. She not only looks back in anger, she exists in a permanent state of all-round fury. Any man who has shared the Great Miz's miserable life, and her much bounced-on bed, can't be a total flop. I rate him as a red-blooded hero just for taking on the dismal, nagging bitch.

Not sharing the Greery Group's sex-searching sorrows, my university life was happily packed. Among my most memorable men friends – we truly were just good friends – was Jeffrey Thomas, president of the University Union, later MP for Abertillery, and now a QC. Jeffrey was the sharpest wit I ever knew, and, at twenty-two, the world's worst dancer, as we discovered on the eve of the university ball, to be graced by our then Chancellor, the Queen Mother. On the night before The Night, I casually remarked, 'The Queen Mum's a terrific dancer, you know, I hope you're up to it.' Jeffrey's limbs began to shake like a strung-up puppet.

'You don't mean I'll have to dance with her?' he said, his harping Welsh voice coming totally unstrung.

'You're the Union president, you berk, you'll have to kick off!'

The kick-off would be literal, he moaned. He couldn't dance on the end of the rope by which he was ready to hang himself rather than face the Queen Mum. Jeff and I took our first out-of-step steps around 9 p.m. By midnight, my bloody and battered feet were twice their size, but he could now waltz, quickstep, and foxtrot as if the Quorn was after him in full cry.

The great night, and the astonishingly small Queen Mum arrived. She waltzed merrily through conversation, but didn't physically stir until the band struck up the Gay Gordons, when she began to tap her tiny, high-heeled foot, and clap her little white-gloved hands. Jeffrey went the colour of her gloves. I longed to escape his accusing eyes, wild with terror, by diving under her vast crinoline. All that blue Scottish blood pounding through the woman's veins, and I'd never thought of the wretched Gay Gordons. There was no escape. 'Do you like the Gay Gordons, Mr Thomas?' foot-tapped the Queen Mum. 'May I have the honour, Ma'am?' he leapt to the feet I prayed wouldn't give way under him.

The first round was reeling slaughter. Not so much the Gay

Gordons as the Glencoe Massacre, with Jeffrey yomping the wrong way down the glen. The pipe band, appalled at the prospect of the Queen Mum in a literal flat spin, squealed to a halt. Silence fell like Jeffrey's flushed face. His royal partner shot a perceptive glance at it, then saved it by clapping her wee white gloves – the royal signal for the band to play on.

By round two, Jeffrey, quick on the uptake, had got the measure, by round three he was into his manly stride, expertly spinning his partner under his outstretched arm, like a turquoise satin top. The wonderful woman ended the dance by gently waving everyone to a halt, and then completing six solo spins, to crashing applause. She crowned our evening by remarking, 'How very clever of you, Mr Thomas, to dance the Gay Gordons without knocking my tiara off!'

My undergraduate days ended on a silver-lined cloud nine. Then I fell heavily for a married man of thirty-six, and nearly broke my heart and nerve. I had been playing harmless games, and always winning, with boys of my own age. Now I met my master, and what I dreamed would be my everlasting match. He opened my eyes, and much more. By dazzling me with glitz like the Coq d'Or and the Dorchester, he shrank all previous suitors to beardless, penniless boys, and, within weeks, I was utterly besotted. And absolutely unable to cope.

On the brink of a divorce, he pushed me over the edge of all common sense by promising marriage. I made huge mountains of passion out of what I later realized was his molehill fancy for a green girl, fresh out of college. Terrified of losing him, I pushed too hard. When I felt him resisting, and backing off, I flattened myself at his feet, inviting the boot. At a final Dorchester tea, he was bored stiff as I was rigid with misery at the realization that it was over. He was slipping away from me, but all I could do was cling on with hurt, losing hands.

He jilted me, brutally, on Doncaster station. On the bleakest winter's night of my life to date, four days before Christmas, we stood huddled against the cold on the platform, but already miles apart. As he waved away my train to Hull, I knew I would never see him again. He never wrote, never rang, never explained.

I'm sure I should tell you he still owns an aching piece of my heart. Not a sliver of it. Maybe I'm incapable of the grand, sacrificial, death-dealing passion women are supposed to suffer at least once in their tremulous lives. Or maybe I'm basically a comic rather than a tragic being. At any rate, I recovered shamefully rapidly, and never pass through Don-caster station without curling up at the *Brief Encounter* scene in which I played a frantic Celia Johnson to a Trevor Howard who didn't want the part.

An only slightly wounded lioness, I planned, in future, to be a heartless man-eater. Then I met Geoff. It was love at first sight, and his was blind. I no longer needed to worry about my image: Geoff saw me as perfect. So blinkered was he by passion, I wonder if he ever really saw me.

One dingy afternoon in Sheffield, desperate for a new head-line for my weekly column, I had my hair died vivid ginger. I looked appalling. At best like a seed packet marigold, at worst like next door's tomcat. Next morning, when sunlight sparked off it, I marvel my hair didn't set alight to my sheets. I blazed like Blake's tiger, only burning brighter. With no time to quench the flames before my 2 o'clock *Sheffield Telegraph* shift, I streaked into the building, like fire through corn, scattering colleagues shrinking from the heat. I stood, shim-mering, in front of the news desk. Geoff looked up without batting an eyelid. 'You're down for the Co-op fashion show,' he said.

'Geoff,' I croaked, parch-lipped, 'look at my hair!' He raised his eyes again and blinked. 'Never mind,' he said, 'it'll grow out.' I knew then that I would marry him.

Next day, I had the hair cooled down to burned copper, and stayed that colour for twenty years, until the silver threads began to gleam through. Geoff never noticed them, either. They could have chopped lumps off without diminishing me in his rose-spectacled eyes. When they actually did chop a lump off me, Geoff said that in his view there was nothing missing. 'It won't grow out this time,' I choked. 'Never mind,' he said. 'I don't.'

My image was restored. Now I'd no excuse for not getting on with it.

CHAPTER ◆ ELEVEN

Back with a Vengeance

*H*aving picked myself up, and stitched my act back together almost as neatly as my healing scar, I was mentally ready to tackle the *Express* again, full time. But if the spirit was willing, the still flushed and sensitive flesh was weak.

What had previously been life's trivial burdens – handbag, briefcase, even a half-empty plastic carrier – now dragged like a job for a fork-lift truck. Being right-handed, I'd always kept my offside free for my door and car keys, and hung any dead weights on my left. Since school satchel-hood, anything with a strap was slotted over my left shoulder. Books, magazines, and my daily ton of newspapers were wedged under my left arm. Supermarket basket handles braceleted my left wrist. To function now, I had to make a drastic change of sides which left me feeling psychologically lop-sided.

Since I was back on the job I'd assured the *Express* I could hold down, I didn't expect them to hand-pick me delicate recuperative chores for the bottom of the woman's page. I just prayed my first test wouldn't be a royal tour of Russia, with

Prince Philip banging on about 'sickle-eyed Soviets', and whipping up World War III.

I'd been back a couple of days when the Duchess of York's father, Major Ronald Ferguson, rang me. Could I have lunch with him at Claridges?

If you know Fergie's sire, the galloping Major Ron, you know where his broad-rumped, red-maned filly of a daughter gets it from. And why she keeps putting her hoof in it with the rest of the more tightly-reined royal family. Long before he fell from his high horse, allegedly caught with his breeches down in a Wigmore Street massage parlour, I'd have bet my shirt that Prince Charles's polo manager was riding flat out for disaster like a snorting runaway stallion. Twice-married, fifty-five, leathery-faced, but still supple as his boots and his polished charm, Ron's impact on women was a one-man Charge of the Light Brigade. It probably still is. I speak of him, sadly, in the past tense because, since he publicly committed social suicide, the royals have tied up Ron's tongue like a skittish polo pony.

But this sexy, sexist old soldier was one of a dying, red-blooded breed. He was not a woman's, but a ladies' man. Women's bloody battle for equality had glanced off Ron like a stray passing bullet. He believed all fillies, and even old grey militant mares, should be snaffled and broken in, and that he should jiggle the reins. With his bristling, built-in busby eyebrows, and his prancing gallantry with every woman who caught his bolting blue eye, a one-to-one interview with Ron was more dangerous than the Grand National. The temptation to slip and fall for his thundering sex appeal was compulsive as having a crack at Becher's Brook to see if you could land on the other side intact.

In March 1986, when his second daughter became engaged to the Queen's second son in a blaze of publicity to match her ruby ring, the Major gave a series of rather stately, tight-lipped statements on TV. As former Commander of the Household Cavalry's Sovereign Escort, Ron could be pompously stiff as his old ceremonial breastplate in those early days before his loosened tongue galloped away with him. I felt he could do better than that, but couldn't wangle an exclusive face-to-face. With one nervous eye on the Queen – his former boss and future sister-in-law – the Major was on a tight rein. He would only preside at formal press conferences on the sacred turf of Windsor's Smith's Lawn, headquarters of the mega-pukka Guards Polo Club.

From the off, Sarah Ferguson looked like taking the cup as the World's Worst Dressed Woman, and America had already handed her it. In painted, dieted, face-lifted Nancy Reagan-land, they didn't understand an earthy, messy, sexy twenty-six-year-old Sloane Ranger. They didn't realize that all well-bred British Sloanes look like Fergie in muddy green wellies, manure colours, no lipstick, sludgey tartans, and lumpy home-made jumpers three sizes too big.

'Frumpy Fergie!' pouted the world's disappointed glossy magazines, who'd hoped for another perfectly pruned, slim-stalked English rose like Princess Diana. I agreed with them, but saw Fergie's earthiness as a plus if she was to hold down Randy Andy, the young naval salt, fresh from a girl in every port, not to mention the now forbidden name, Koo Stark.

As wedding fever mounted, I led my weekly column, head-lined 'Fergie *is* a Frump' with:

> Sarah Ferguson looks like an unbrushed red setter strug-gling to get out of a hand-knitted potato sack. She also looks great fun, powerfully sexy, tremendously boisterous and thrilling to men. Fergie may dress like a tumbledown Eng-lish cottage, covered with a lichen-coloured cardigan, but this huge handful of an energetic, romping girl could make Randy Andy very happy.

This made Fergie ecstatic, and her father rang to tell me so. Unlike real royals, who snootily make it as difficult as possible for you to write the radiant eight-page colour sup-plement they expect when they get married, the Fergusons, still warm-hearted commoners, were touchingly pleased with praise.

Having slipped a halter on the Major, I wasn't about to let

him bolt off the phone. What about a private tea party on Smith's Lawn? He agreed, and gave me what proved to be near fatal directions to the polo club. Glamorously streaking through deserted Windsor Great Park in my Jaguar, I took a wrong turning, and was breathtaken by my sudden, gloriously uninterrupted view of the Golden Mile – the Queen's strictly private carriageway between Windsor Castle and Ascot race-course. I'd never seen it from the top end before. Within seconds, I could see nothing but an armoured van in front, and two agitatedly wailing police cars behind. I was parked a bomb's throw from the Queen's dining room window, and she was lunching at home. My arrival at Guards with an armed escort nearly unseated the Major, who had to bail me out of my surrounded Jag.

The Major's mood matched the sunny April day. As we sat in dampish deckchairs on the very polo lawn where, thirteen years previously, his first wife Susan, Sarah's mother, met and bolted with the dashing Argentine polo player, Hector Barrantes, Ron's tongue began to trot, canter, and then fly like the final furlong of The Derby. Once opened up, he let it all flow like the tears he told me he expected to shed, escorting his daughter on her final, four-minute, red-carpeted walk up Westminster Abbey's aisle, and into the royal family his family had served for years. 'One doesn't want to cry in public with millions watching on TV, but I'm sure I shall, and I really don't see any harm in a man's tears, they're a wonderful relief of emotion,' said the Major, dismounting from his high horse, his stiff upper lip softening for the first time.

Nobody would notice him anyway, he gambled, now that Prince Andrew had made the startling decision to allow a camera to face a royal couple, for the first time in history, at the magic moment they took their vows. 'They've obviously thought a lot about that camera – first it was off, then on again – and I'm a bit surprised they finally agreed to share their vows with the whole world,' he said, a touch wistful and shocked. 'Still, among all those cameras I suppose another one won't make much difference, and Sarah wanted to share her day with everyone. She's a great girl for making everybody happy. I'll be talking to her every step of the way up the aisle, of course.'

I reminded him that, when Prince Philip gave away Princess Anne, the expert lip readers hired by TV latched straight on to 'You're sure you're all right?' and 'This is it, here we go.' 'Since I'm told I don't open my mouth when I speak, even the lip readers won't know what I say to her,' the Major smiled. 'And she'll be nagging the dear old geriatric Dad all the way. It'll start in the carriage – I can hear it now – with "Dad, sit there, get out of the way, don't move, you're taking up too much room", and it'll go on all the way until she reaches Prince Andrew.'

In an interview a few weeks after the wedding that was watched by 800 million in thirty countries, I asked for a replay of what was actually said on the day. 'In the coach, it took us a while to get used to talking to each other, facing the other way, and waving out of the window,' Fergie's father recalled. 'About half way down Whitehall I nudged her and said "Just look at all those people; why are they here? All come to see my smelly little daughter." She nearly fell about, hissing "Shut up, Dad!"'

Did he shed a tear? 'Yes, when I first saw her in that dress with the Ophelia flowers in her hair. I'd made a pact with Sarah not to tell me anything about the dress, and not to let me see her until just before the TV viewers did. At her big moment, I wanted to be like everyone else, completely surprised. When I heard the door of Clarence House open, and there she was, it was breathtaking, there's no other word.

'I thought of saying all sorts of things to calm her down – well, to calm me down – and then I saw the happiness and confidence in her face, and I knew we'd have no trouble. When somebody trod on her train and she let out a good swear word, I thought "everything's as normal, we're home and dry".' This was the man caught bending by the world's cameras to straighten Fergie's eighteen-foot train at the abbey door. 'What the hell, I was her father on her biggest day. If her dress wasn't right, it was the most natural thing in the world to stoop down and pull it out.

'But I'll tell you one thing that did feel incredibly unreal
. . . riding in that coach with the Queen after the number of
times I've ridden beside it on a horse,' said the ex-Cavalry
Commander to whom the Queen once joked, 'Back a bit, Ron,
they've come to see me, not you.'

Outpourings like this endeared Fergie Senior to my readers,
and to me. The man seemed upright and well balanced,
particularly in his dislike of odious comparisons between size
sixteen Fergie and the size ten Princess of Wales, and even
rasher analogies between our virgin future Queen Diana on
her wedding day, and the redheaded Duchess who invited two
of her old flames, old Etonian Kim Smith-Bingham, and
motor racing manager, Paddy McNally, to join in the Abbey
fun.

'They can't skinny Sarah down to the model-girl size of the
Princess of Wales. She is what she is – she hasn't the bone
structure to diet away six or seven stones,' he snapped. 'And
I get very cross at unfair comparisons between Diana's shyness
at first and Sarah's self-confidence. At twenty-six, Sarah jolly
well should be more street-wise than a girl who was nineteen
when she married.

'As for former romances, would you expect any normal girl
of twenty-six not to have had romances, and, if she hadn't,
wouldn't people wonder why? Can you see Prince Andrew
choosing a girl of twenty-six no other man had looked at?
Even the Queen Mother said, "Of course a girl of twenty-six
will have had previous boyfriends,"' he neatly invoked the
most sacred name in the royal family. Anything the Queen
Mum says, goes.

This had all been good, lively, but discreet stuff, crowned
by the Major's rather stuffy insistence on calling his son-in-law
'Sir'. 'Prince Andrew is Prince Andrew. After twenty-two
years as a soldier, I find nothing odd in calling him "Sir",
and wouldn't dream of "Andrew". The only thing I would
find odd would be behaving in the reverse,' said righteous
Ron, clanking with patriotism like his medals.

Now, a year later, this richly regal stuff was wearing thin.
The overweight, overbearing Duke and Duchess of Pork were

gaining poundage, and losing popularity by the hour. Fergie's flamboyantly dressed tour of America had been a disaster in appalling taste, as her father was the first to admit when I met him at our Claridges lunch. Grieved as he was by my calling his darling daughter 'our disastrous Duchess', Ron was honestly bound to agree that blinding Los Angeles with the diamante letters 'LA' on the band of a black hat bigger than Clint Eastwood's had been a dazzling error. 'Not to mention those dreadful diamante American flags and Union Jacks she ran up the back of her hair-do like morse code,' groaned Ron. 'God knows I've tried to warn her what a mess she looks at times. That thing she wore at Ascot right at the start with the stripes going round the wrong way turned her into a balloon. I thought it was absolutely terrible, so I rang her up and said so.'

Isn't it true that 'Sir' eggs on his wife to look what he considers 'sexy and striking', and the world thinks is making a fashion fool of herself? Prince Andrew's taste, let's face it, is about as subtle as a sat-on whoopee cushion. Ron wasn't going to face that, but he flushed the shade of his smoked salmon at my hint that her husband could be at the big, ungirdled bottom of Fergie's ever increasing fashion problems, enlarging by the day now that she was hugely pregnant.

He'd asked me to lunch to invite me to join his party at a gala charity performance, in the presence of the Yorks, of Barry Humphries' smash-hit West End show, *Back with a Vengeance*. I'd already seen the show, and knew just how vengeful it was, from the swearing, spitting, slobbering opening by the repellent Sir Les Patterson, Australia's cultural ambassador, to the climactic close in which Dame Edna Everage picks six victims from her audience, and publicly crucifies them on stage.

'I think Barry's going to have me up there doing something silly,' beamed the Major, as a major organizer of the event. The Queen's brother-in-law, waving a gladiola? I sweated for him. This now publicity-mad man made the Charge of the Light Brigade look like careful strategy.

Barry Humphries is an old mate of mine, and one of my

The dear old boobs in sunnier days.

Left: No Kidding!

Above: Hold that tiger!

Below: Ben Her.

Above: Mum, me and the Milky Bar Kid.

Below: South Riding.

The young Etonian.

Friend and
protector, Jo.

'You can tell 'em the "ebony" panthers are really only concrete glass fibre.' When this final reel was taken by the *Express*, I never told them that Diana was losing her battle against cancer and was broke.

Left: Back with a vengeance — Major Ron's last performance.

Right: With the eternal Barbara Cartland.

Above: Gresby practises his up-chat on a sex queen, Jackie Collins.

Below: That's not my toy boy, that's my boy!

favourite people. Or three people, depending if he's wearing his own off-stage homburg, Les Patterson's protruding false fangs, or Edna's wisteria wig. When he'd sent me tickets for his show the first time I saw it, shortly after Christmas, I'd sent an urgent note back-stage. 'For God's sake don't pull me out of the audience tonight, I could fall flat at your feet,' I wrote, foreseeing myself lying on stage under a pall of gladdies.

Dressing for the gala night was another test of my healing body's endurance. Could it take the strain of the tight, plunging black bra I needed under a low-necked black evening dress that clung to what used to be my curves? After a battle royal between the snappish bra and my unbalanced boobs, I was cheered that I still looked curved in what looked like all the right places still in their right place. The black bra felt murderously like Julius Caesar's breastplate, buckled too tight, but the effect, after weary weeks under wraps, sheets, and sloppy cotton shirts, was stunning.

The celebrity audience in the first five rows of the packed Strand theatre on gala night was as flashy as Elton John's £15,000 diamond earring, glittering under his French onion-seller's black beret. As Dame Edna raked us with her two-pronged eyes, Elton was calming the nervous, and himself, with 'She can only pick out people in light colours in the first two rows.' I knew he was three rows short, and that Edna's rhinestone specs can pinpoint her victims in the dark.

Paula Yates, on the front-row firing line, was clinging like a petrified platinum koala to her husband's hair. Since Geldof had earlier taken the full sprinkler force of Sir Les Patterson's spitting, she kept slipping off. Geldof accused Billy Connelly, bellowing his beard off in the rocking seat behind mine, of 'laughing like a sycophant so she won't pick on you'. Connelly's live-in lover, Pamela Stephenson, due to give birth the week before Fergie, was sheltering from Edna's impending storm of abuse in a flowered maternity marquee big enough to hold a wedding party.

Fergie and Andy, no fools, were perched in the dress circle out of reach of the Dame's blood-red claws. Rooted as I wished I was to my seat with terror at what we all knew was coming,

I thanked God that I'd be the last to be picked. Compared with Edna's five-row herbaceous border of Britain's most blooming showbiz talent, I was but an insignificant Fleet Street weed. But since I guessed there was no way out (Edna bars the exits) for the set-up Major Ron, I could have spat like Sir Les when Ron asked me to sit next to him. We shrivelled in our seats like blighted gladdies as Edna started to pluck her prey from the audience.

Like forked lightning, she struck a non-celebrity lady called 'Di' ('my favourite way of spelling it, possum'). Then an unknown Eileen, an unsung Roz, and a hapless latecomer got it in the neck. The celebrities began to perk up in their £200 seats. Edna publicly executes only six people nightly, so, with Fergie's father to go, that left only one whose lurching heart was about to be attacked.

Innocent gladdie that I was, I never dreamed of it even in my wildest nightmares. 'What's your name, dear?' asked Edna, her scarlet neon specs boring into me like a pair of heat-seeking missiles. 'The blond woman second in from the left?' Please God let it be Judith Chalmers, in the seat in front. 'Not her, dear, *you*,' Edna snapped like an outback crocodile. 'What's your name? Jeeeeeean!' she made it sound endless as the inescapable torment to come. She stripped my outfit, my hair-do, my bedroom on which she insisted on a wall-to-wall description – 'And do you have mirrors on your red ceiling, Jeeeeean?'

I'd interviewed Edna four tottering times, and Barry Humphries twice. If ever I dragged Barry out of Edna again, I'd kill him. By hand.

Then, 'Who's the little senior person you've brought with you, dear?' Edna's voice whispered wickedly round the rocking gallery. I realized, with horror, that Fergie's father and I were about to die shoulder to shoulder. We were trapped. Locking the now very nervous Ron by the wrist, I tripped over my too-long dress up the six stairs to the scaffold.

Swept into the wings for a 'fancy dress party', I was pushed back into the spotlight in a four-foot cock feather headdress and feather cape, looking like Carmen Miranda freshly dug up. Major Ron was even more appallingly fitted out as an aged punk with a puce Mohican hair-cut, and a black leather Hell's Angel jacket, rattling with swastikas and metal chains.

'Lucky possum that you are, you are now a mini star!' shrieked Edna, handing me a bottle of pink Aussie champagne, and the Major a tub of Vaseline. Hurling a few parting flowery insults at us, she began boomeranging gladdies into the ecstatic audience. As Edna tossed them to the furthest row of the gallery, Barry's muscles, in her backless dress, stood out like snakeskin whipcords.

'I can hit a royal in the eye at twenty-five yards,' he muttered in my ear, burning with the grilling heat from the footlights, and ringing with applause. 'Keep smiling and throwing, possum. After all you've been through, my God, am I glad to see you on this stage tonight.'

I was thrilled myself, albeit hysterically, that my remaining good right arm was good enough to wing Bob Geldof with a happy gladdie. I wouldn't live through this nightmare night again if they gave me Australia studded with diamonds the size of Elton John's earring, but I felt thankful that I'd managed to keep my end and my strength up in what had to be the ultimate physical test.

Standing alongside him, I still had this uneasy feeling that the Duchess of York's father, in a puce punk wig, was playing with the chop. It came, as sharp as Charles I's, the following weekend. The Major's risky stage appearance faded beside his total exposure, allegedly down to his bare buttocks, in front page tabloid horror stories of 'The Major and the Massage Girls' and 'Fergie's Father in Den of Vice'.

Randy Ron's lunch hours, trumpeted the *Sun*, had been spent working out, and not in a gym. He'd enjoyed having his bare bottom oiled and slapped, in ticklish situations in a well-known massage parlour. What stunned about these stories, which the Major didn't deny, was his blinkered naïvety. Strings of famous showbiz, sporting and political clients of the notorious Wigmore Club crawled in by its back door. But not our Ronald, who virtually courted getting caught.

Riding along on his charger, allegedly over blondes and redheads alike, 'Fergie Senior' as he was known and loved by the shady ladies of Wigmore, was as proud as an Indian Rajah of his royal connections. 'How does it feel to be dealing with royalty?' he was said to have playfully rump-slapped as he banged down his briefcase, emblazoned with his full real name with which, several years previously, he'd enrolled as a club member. Never furtive Ron, hammering on the front door with his fiery hooves, had all but snorted 'Hey, hey, clear the way, I am the galloping Major!'

A few frantic hours after his Grand National fall, I got a phone call. 'You'll have seen it?' said Ron. Ron, I said, it's what's known as blanket coverage – unless you were dead to the world, you couldn't miss it. 'I've been an ass, haven't I?' said the fallen cavalry man. A fool to the point of madness, but a likeable one.

'Did you see that hilarious cartoon in the *Sun*?' Ron asked, bringing me out in a nervous sweat, like the perspiring smiling steed in the picture, stretched out on a massage couch, in the grip of a topless blonde, with the caption 'We don't see the Major any more, but his horse is still a regular customer.' 'I saw it, Ron,' I hedged, not wanting to believe what I was about to hear. 'You didn't. . . .'

'I wrote off for it!' neighed the triumphant galloping Major. 'Why not?'

'Because they'll print your letter!' I snapped, exasperated by the man's obsession with riding into the jaws of death.

'They wouldn't, would they? Oh Christ!' It was as good a prayer as any, but hopeless.

Next morning's *Sun* blazoned the cartoon on its front page, with a letter headed 'Guards Polo Club – President HRH Prince Philip, Duke of Edinburgh', and signed Ronald Ferguson. 'I would be grateful if I could have either the original or a copy of your excellent cartoon in today's paper, 10th May,' wrote Ron. Hell bent on the knacker's yard, he added, 'I thank you for your co-operation in advance.'

There was nothing I, or any of his many genuine friends in the press, could write to save Ron's broken neck. Rapidly nudged out of the Guards Club, all he could do was ride into his social sunset. These days, sadly, we seldom hear a whinny from the galloping Major. The British monarch may no longer have the power to put traitors to The Family's image in the Tower. But she can still slam down the portcullis on their silenced tongues.

CHAPTER ◆ TWELVE

The Making of Maggie

*T*o brag that I 'discovered' Margaret Thatcher would be like claiming Tutankhamun's treasure didn't exist until somebody bashed a hole in a wall and tripped over it. Or that Victoria Falls's seventy-five million gallons-per-minute were turned on like a tap, seconds before Livingstone walked round a bush to be drowned in disbelief.

Nobody 'finds' a phenomenon like Thatcher. But somebody had to spot her, and her potential, at her surprisingly shaky start. Exclusively among British journalists who, fifteen years ago, had scarcely seen her, and foreign scribes who'd never heard of her, I claim that alone I did it. I was so alone when I predicted in print, in 1974, 'Margaret Thatcher has it in her to become Britain's first woman prime minister,' that even Maggie herself was then hedging, 'I foresee a woman PM, but not in my lifetime,' and crumpled-up colleagues were falling about with, 'You can't mean that powder-puff blonde from North Finchley who wears those bloody stupid hats?'

I'll admit my own words to my news desk, on the Friday afternoon when I rang for an interview with Mrs Thatcher in February 1974 – no appointment needed, and she answered the phone herself – were, 'I'm a touch short of election material, so I'll slip up to Finchley and write a few paras on that Tory blonde in those hats.'

Ten minutes into the interview, I was eating my words with the Marks and Sparks biscuits Maggie still carries with her round the world. At hard centre, the sugary pink and white Mrs Thatcher was not just a tough cookie. Cross her and, even then, you risked smashing a tooth.

'If you picture me as a fluffy-minded blonde, graciously arranging roses in her fifty-foot lounge, I shall be mad,' warned the English rose who, in her dew-drenched days, looked like a long-stemmed, thornless pink bud, still in its cellophane wrapper. 'I can't help being blonde – if your hair was mouse brown with grey bits at the side, you'd tint it – and I can't help having a fair skin and looking clean. But I get wild with people who don't realize that, under all this' – she tapped her porcelain bosom – 'there's a bit of tough steel that's me.'

That was the first recorded clank from the future Iron Lady. In my next nine interviews, over fifteen years, I was to watch Maggie forge herself into a cutting edge that blunts Excalibur to a rusty razor blade. Give her another decade, no doubt still in office, and she will have self-soldered into a solid bronze bust they can mount straight on to her waiting plinth in Westminster.

But in those distant days when we first met, Mrs Thatcher was far from political *crème de la crème*. In fact her first taste of fame had been sour. As Education Secretary in the 1970–74 Heath government, she had curdled the nation by ending free school milk, and then lost her bottle at public, tomato-chucking chants of 'Thatcher, Thatcher, Milk Snatcher!' by choking ('though I never actually cried' the PM claims to this day): 'You don't know what it's like when everybody hates you.'

These days, Mighty Margaret could smash milk bottles with her left hand while she KO's Kinnocks with her strong right. But we all have to start somewhere . . . as I said to myself in 1974, toiling up the uncarpeted stairs to her Finchley office, then about the size of a milk float. The bosomy blonde behind the desk hardly bigger than a dispatch box greeted me with, 'I remember what you wrote in your column at the time of the "milk snatching" incident' – Maggie's favourite ploy, even way back, was to rob journalists speechless by snatching the words out of their mouths. 'You said, "Mrs Thatcher should stop crying into her initialled lace hankie that she's the Most Unpopular Girl in the Fifth, show some spunk, and hit them back." I didn't forget that.'

She has never forgotten it. Wonder Woman not only hit back. Within a decade, she had slaughtered Ted Heath's political career, crushed Callaghan, become Prime Margaret, and bloodily annihilated Labour, the Liberals, and the S.D.P.

The afternoon before Ted Heath's blood bath, in 1975, I was taking tea and the inevitable M and S biscuits with the woman who was about to axe him by cutting the Tory leadership from under his feet. Nobody else wanted to interview her. Male-edited Fleet Street was secure that Ted would win the leadership election. The *Daily Express*, under Alastair Burnet, had laid on oceans of champers to toast Sailor Heath, and Ted himself was to call at the *Express* building around midnight to be launched on his merrily bobbing next four years.

I was still backing my strong, if somewhat solitary, hunch that Thatcher would win. That fateful afternoon, since Maggie's office in the House of Commons was then only a biscuit's throw from Ted's, we spoke in lowered voices. Maggie was already working on dropping hers an octave, since she worried about her platform performance. 'I can hear my voice getting higher and more screechy, and I keep telling myself, "Keep it down!"' I kept mine down because Ted was, and still is, a personal chum; and, as I felt bound to mention to Maggie, in supporting her in print against him, I felt like the hottest traitor to visit Parliament since Guy Fawkes.

'I know what you mean,' she said, with that stunningly sincere habit she'd already developed of leaning into her interviewer, her face furrowed with concern, like a nurse about to bandage your finger. Then she prophetically added, in her new, softly confiding voice, like a cello played at the wrong speed on a wound-down gramophone: 'I'll always be fond of dear Ted, but there's no personal sympathy in politics.'

The minute she said that, I knew Ted was politically dead. Hours later, the rest of a very flustered Fleet Street was burying him. Thatcher had wiped Heath off the front bench as if with a feather duster.

She dusts a lot, incidentally. Interviewing her, even these days, is always made hectic by her housewifely habit of plumping up No. 10's cushions, and vacuuming under the Chippendale with her eyes, even while she's tidying up a world crisis in conversation.

On the 250th anniversary of the opening of 10 Downing Street, six years after she moved in, Maggie invited me round for coffee and a conducted tour. I'm always disappointed you don't get to bang the brass lion knocker on the world's most photographed front door, but only to rap lightly on one of the policemen posted outside. This particular rainy day, the black-and-white-tiled front hall, perfect for playing draughts, was suicidally slippery, but I cringed to set wet foot on Maggie's priceless Persian carpets.

'I don't mind muddy feet so much as people who come to receptions and drop crumbs and little cocktail sticks all over the floor,' warned my hostess. To avoid any slips, I quickly put down yet another of her obligatory bloody biscuits on a handy plate which turned out to be William Pitt's priceless solid silver gilt salver. 'Don't worry too much, the carpet in here isn't original. I was terrified when we moved in and they told me the most valuable thing in the house was a Persian carpet worth half a million. I mean, anything worth that lot shouldn't be put on the floor,' she said, from the house-proud heart which still throbs inside her statesman's steel breast-plate.

'So I got the British Museum experts in, and when they took one look and said they'd got the original and ours was just a copy, it was quite a relief. The value went down dramatically, but at least we dare tramp on the thing again. Museums are very good about helping out. When I walked into this place it looked like "furnished house to let". Would you believe there wasn't an ornament, not a thing, on any flat surface? All the wonderful things I've got dotted on tables and mantelpieces are borrowed. Museums and art galleries lend things.'

Gladly? 'No, it has to be prised out of them.' Maggie shot me the look she gives Gorbachev on arms deals, 'and you don't always get what you expect. When I asked for something for my little Science Corridor, they sent me a bust of Michael Farady on a granite plinth weighing three-quarters of a ton. We had to leave him downstairs, or he'd have crashed through the floor.'

I had the impression Maggie would rather be carried out of No. 10 than move to poor old husband Denis's Dulwich dream home, a short putt from a golf course, bought by the Thatchers in the unlikely event that she'll lose an Election, or retire.

'I dread leaving,' she told me earnestly. 'You never get over living in a house which has seen so much history, and I'm still as thrilled as the day we moved in. It's an address everyone knows, and one of the first things you hear about as a child,' enthused the little Grantham girl whom some suspect painted 'No. 10' on her doll's house.

Actually, the overall effect of this surprisingly small, if super semi-detached, with its silk-walled rooms crammed with priceless objets and lit by three-foot rock crystal chandeliers, is somewhat stuffy. Not to say static as a Sunday colour supplement and hushed as Gladstone's deaf aid. Or it would be, were it not for Maggie bustling around like a permanently new broom, and flicking about like the feather duster she still carries.

The first woman-about-the-house given by George II to Sir Robert Walpole in 1735, isn't overawed by her predecessors. Or miffed by being followed to bed, up the portrait-lined stairs, by the eyes of forty-eight men besides Denis. Disraeli's startling likeness looks poised to leap from his frame, but the only past PM who disturbs her is James Callaghan, who broke with the house's sober tradition of black and white photos only, and had himself snapped in colour. What worries Maggie is not that Callaghan gaily clashes with the rest of British history, but that he's fading. 'I warned him colour would fade – he's going so fast, one day he'll disappear,' she said, anxiously tapping Jim's glass like a barometer. 'I really must ring up and have a word with him about it.'

The PM is no mere sitting tenant. She personally stripped the flocked paper off the study, regardless of the history seen by the long-gone flies on the wall. 'It was a sickly sage green, it closed in on me, I couldn't stand it, and the house is dark enough as it is, even on a sunny day, so I paid for the new silvery wallpaper myself.'

With the hands which help to shape the western world, Maggie hurled Mrs Stanley Baldwin's settees on to the scrap heap with the vigour with which Mrs Baldwin's husband chucked out Edward VIII. 'They were absolutely enormous things in tatty gold silk, but, mercifully for me, the springs went.' And she and Denis did a midnight 'to you, from me' removal of a vastly hideous cupboard at the top of the stairs, in which Lloyd George probably kept his skeletons. 'You can still see the marks where the thing stood. I came down every night for weeks with my little kitchen knife, but I've never managed to get them all out.'

At the top of No. 10, you burst through the mists of history into Maggie's and Denis's startlingly bright, white painted little world of their own. It's only a humble attic conversion – sitting room, three mini bedrooms, boxroom, matchbox kitchen and the usual – but to Maggie, there's no place like it.

It's here she kicks off her PM-ship like a pair of too-tight shoes. 'These are *my* things,' she points out, her eyes caressing more than three decades of marriage – the framed photos of the twins, Mark and Carol ('I can't wait to be a grandmother, I've felt so deprived not being able to baby-sit') and her carefully glass-cased Crown Derby which 'Denis and I collected, bit by bit, over ages.' In pride of place is a plate, crudely depicting her head, and apparently Made in Margate, lovingly mounted on a Woolworths bracket. 'The Chinese gave it to me – wasn't it sweet of them? It's so cleverly made, even if it does make me look a bit fat, and you can't wash it in case it runs.'

This is the softer side of the Iron Lady few but her family see. The day she ate Ted Heath alive, nobody could even glimpse what the Tories saw in their new leaderette, least of all Ted, who mulishly refused to take it in. Portly, pink-chopped 'dear Ted' is essentially a chauvinist bachelor who believes that a woman's place is in any man's home but his, or, if she must worry her pretty little head about politics, she should sit still on the back bench, preferably with a tin of polish.

Heath was totally blasted by Thatcher's victory. For forty-eight hours he was in shock, like a man who'd been playing with a kitten when it grew overnight into a jugular-slitting jaguar. Finally shorn of all power, he turned nastier than Samson, and began shaking the Tory temple round their ears. When it didn't crack, he foot-stamped so petulantly, I was goaded to lead my column with, 'Just because he can't sit at the head of the table any more, Ted Heath really shouldn't spoil the Party by childishly pulling Margaret's hair and hurling the jellies about.'

Outraged Ted sent me a glacial letter, followed by an even frostier Christmas card, signed 'Edward Heath', from which I gathered I was deeply in it. It was several springs before he thawed out, and invited me to house-warm his exquisitely tasteful Home and Garden, so close to Salisbury Cathedral its spire looks like one of his cypress trees. At home, Ted is witty and charming to women, leading Olivia de Havilland to speculate on TV: 'Why isn't he married? – I'd marry him like a shot!' But in the House, he is sullenly sexist, and detests Maggie with a killing loathing.

That day she filched his job, a vast percentage of Britain's voters shared Heath's dislike of the 'haughty Tory Lady Bountiful', and she knew it. 'I've a lot to offer,' she told me. 'I've fantastic stamina, great physical strength, and a woman's ability to stick with a job and get on with it when everyone else walks off and leaves it. But there's something about me that loses votes.' I hoped she wouldn't ask me to put my pen on just what. 'I already know, it's the "flawless" skin and the "condescending" voice, and you're right about the "gracious Tory Lady" bit, because That Look comes all too easily to me, and it's a worry.' Schoolgirl Margaret's hooow-nooow-brooown-cooow elocution lessons were her father's worst-spent money. The Grantham grocer's daughter might know her onions, but how was she to convince the country, sounding like a mouthful of plums?

'I'm trying to drop The Voice because I pipe up too shrilly when I'm nervous, but since my style is "reasonable argument and keep your cool" I'm frightened of pauses. I can hear myself tightening up, getting on one monotonous note, and speaking too loudly and s-l-o-w-l-y,' she boomed at me like Big Ben in urgent need of winding. Even on the brink of PM-ship, four years later, she was still fretting at the tonsillitic tones which irritated her grated ears as much as the voters'. 'I need to be less ponderous and more emotional when I'm speaking to camera. I feel what I'm saying and, when the camera's not there, I say it as I feel it. But once they switch on, I clam up and look a bit aloof and cold.'

These days, of course, Mighty Margaret shuts up Robin Day and the listening nation with 'MAAAaaay I finish?' and her only trace of nerves is a croaking little cough when she knows she's made a good point. Since the cough is amplified by her dozens of mikes, her major speeches sound as if they were recorded on a tropical night creaking with bullfrogs. The second she reads this, Maggie will hire a voice expert to clear the frogs out of the swamp as swiftly as she wound up her delivery after her first disastrous TV talk to the nation in 1975. That night, she went down like a warped violin with viewers who thought she'd been taped and played back at the wrong speed.

Oxford-educated Maggie is not a barrister and chemist for nothing. Within days, she'd changed her style of appeal, and re-mixed her TV phrasing. And she quickly latched on to what turns voters off. She doffed the hats which made cartoon headlines, unpinned the flash brooch from her left lapel ('Who does she think she is, the Queen?') and had her Goldilocks cut and straightened 'When I saw myself on telly one night and noticed how it parted in the middle at the back – awful, but what woman spends her life looking at the back of her head?'

Former TV producer turned Conservative Party public relations man, Gordon Reece, later knighted for his efforts, was the Pygmalion who chipped at Thatcher's coldly marble image by luring her into M and S suits, and on to Radio Two's chuckle 'n chat Jimmy Young Prog. Since the off-the-plastic-hanger suits were a squeeze, she dieted, and still has to: 'When I can't make it into an M & S size 14, I know I'm in trouble.' Her slightly shark-like smile was capped, and there was whiff of a nose job, though Maggie herself assures me her recent answer to a voter who wrote to ask where she'd had her face lifted was, 'It hasn't fallen – yet.'

The Making of Maggie was calculated from the start – probably along with the books above the grocer's shop. Once she hit the prime time, it was computerized by Saatchi and Saatchi until that 'wobbly Thursday' before the last election, when they got the push for failing to rise to the misty glamour of Labour's election sell of Neil and Glenys Kinnock, hand in hand on a cliff top. Rumour has it that Maggie herself, suicidally depressed by the sight of the Caring Kinnocks among heavenly clouds of thrilled seagulls, jumped on Saatchi from a great height.

But even now, she flinches from personally monitoring the Maggie Making. 'I hate watching myself on telly. In the old days, I left it to Denis while I wrote my speeches – I always got a good idea of what was going on when I heard him yelling "*Liars!*" and "That's not *true*, you bastards!" when anyone contradicted me.' The night she first forced herself to study herself, she immediately untied her once trademark pussy bows, admitting that critical viewers were not just being catty: 'They were right, I looked too complicated and fussed.'

In May 1979, on the eve of her election, when the Woman of Destiny felt ready as she would ever be to make British political history, she told me, 'I'll survive if I win because you don't stop to think how you'll do the job, you just turn on the adrenalin and get on with it. I'll survive if I lose, because I'll pick myself up, dust myself off, and soldier on, as women always do. But in my heart, at the bottom of me, I think I'll be Prime Minister.'

In the four years since she'd wooed and won the Tory party, still looking as indecisive as a blonde Barbara Cartland virgin, she'd changed drastically. At fifty-three, she was still very pretty – at sixty-three, come to that, she still is – with her wild rose complexion and pale, kingcup hair. The patronizing headmistress voice was still a hang-up: 'I get so cross with people who say I sound "snobbish", I just wish I could meet them all and get rid of this ridiculous image of the "posh" southern lady who wouldn't win a vote up north.' But she at least sounded less like a seventy-eight rpm recording of Mendelssohn's Violin Concerto, played at thirty-three.

She still had this habit of sidling round the door with her head on one side, like a seed-seeking budgie, but the drooping eyelids were now hooded like a peregrine falcon's. Her soaring ambition was out in the open, and you realized, once in the job, she would spread steel-tipped talons and a sky-sweeping wing span. Her last words to me, in Opposition, were, 'If I don't get in, what will hurt will be the thought of the waste.'

In a lifetime of interviewing every film, stage, political and pop star worth mentioning, the only autographs I'd collected were John Wayne's, Ronnie Reagan's, Princess Grace of Monaco's, and Joan and Jackie Collins's, Koo Stark's, and Britt Ekland's for Gresby, who got a whole new slant on sex at fifteen when Britt signed her picture to him, 'from *the* Older Woman!' Now I asked Maggie to sign a picture we'd taken of her sitting in the middle of a field, fondling a calf – in the foreplay to an election, politicians will kiss anything. 'I'll sign it next week if I get in,' she smiled.

'No, now, my early faith is unshaken,' I grinned back.

I sat up all night to watch Thatcher engulf the map of Britain like a landslide. Four days later, when I greeted fully-made Maggie with 'Good morning, Prime Minister,' she said, 'Strange how, when you get a big job, your good friends stop calling you by your first name.' 'Thanks, Margaret,' I said, thinking she mightn't want to know that, out of earshot, everyone called her 'Maggie'.

In fact she was thrilled when 'Mrs Thatcher' or 'Margaret' at chummiest, went with the wind of change towards her which had swept the country, and public and Press openly nicknamed her 'Maggie'. The title pleased her almost as much as the PM-ship. 'I like being called "good old Maggie!" It's a term of affection, it's rather homely, and it's shorter for newspaper headlines – you've such a job making "Margaret" fit.'

Maggie can be a good sport, although she plays none: 'Since I can't take a sunshine holiday – I just go red and blotchy, and, even as a girl, I never managed brown legs – I was sorry to have to give up the skiing trips we used to take when the twins were younger, but who needs a Prime Minister with a broken leg?' she once sighed when I asked about her barely existent private life. 'I've no time for fun, I'm very dull, really, I'd love to take up tennis with Denis because two can play.' When I lobbed her, 'It's never too late,' she shot back 'Can't you just see 300 cameras focussed on Maggie's shorts?'

At her most sporting, she invited me and TV impersonator, Janet Brown, to tea at the House of Commons. Jan, a lifelong pal of mine, does a shatteringly mirror-like Maggie imitation which has earned her the title 'the Prime Mimicker'. Wigged-up, with her eyebrows pencilled into upside down horseshoes, Jan's such a spitting image of the PM that the American TV channel, NBC, once wickedly set up a spoof meeting between her and the acid-mouthed comedienne, Joan Rivers, in the VIP lounge of Kennedy airport.

NBC dried up Miss Rivers's complaints that she was being held up for her plane by explaining that Britain's prime minister was coming through the lounge, and then sent in Jan, surrounded by security guards and ace American press. 'I was terrified she'd see through me right away, but she swallowed it hook, line and sinker,' snorted Jan who, as Mock Maggie, rounded on Rivers and charged her with 'going far too far with our royal family'. Rivers, gushing apologies and trickling with terror, sprinted across the VIP carpet, spluttering, 'But Mrs Thatcher . . . really, Mrs Thatcher, I didn't mean to offend. . . .'

'I will say Joan took it marvellously,' Jan told me. 'When the TV crew handed her a letter from Johnnie Carson, explaining it was all a gag, there was this terrible silence, as if she'd gone numb and it was taking hours to progress from her stomach to her brain. Then, when they showed her the tape of her making a cringeing fool of herself in front of me, she flung back her head laughing, and shrieking, "Show it, show it, coast to coast! If I dish it out, I must take it!"'

Jan, who admits, 'Maggie crowned my career – I worry almost as much as she does that she'll lose an election and I'll be out of a job,' was hectically flustered when we arrived for our Commons tea. In her nervous excitement, she'd forgotten the padding she always wears because 'Mrs T's got more up top than I have,' and now had two pairs of my tights stuffed down her bra. Getting Thatcher's twin through the Commons lobby wasn't easy. Half the people milling around swore Janet was Brown, the rest nudged that she was Thatcher, and, either way, they wanted her autograph.

Since Jan had often given me a moan by drone demonstration of precisely how she impersonates Maggie, I was nearly hysterical watching the pair meet. Especially when Maggie sprang back, startled as if she'd bumped into her looking glass, with, 'Now, look heeeeere, Miss Brooown [any minute, I thought, she'll add the 'hooow', nooow' and 'co-oow'], I don't speak as slooooowly as that, you make me sound like a run-down car battery.'

Afterwards, Jan told me, 'Talk about the making of Maggie – she's done wonders with herself since I started on her as Tory leader. Her delivery's so much sharper, and she's finally stopped her worst habit of dropping the ends of her sentences. In the old days, her sentences fell off the edge of a cliff where normal people go up. You or I, for instance, would look out of that window and say, "Look at that beautiful tree." Mrs T. used to say, "Now, look at that beautiful TREEEeee . . . eee." She's wound herself up like a spring to stop doing that.

'Some things haven't changed over the years. When you

ask her a question notice how she'll listen to you intently, as if she can't quite catch it, and then drop her eyebrows – everything about her comes from under her eyebrows – and shoot you dead with her answer. She's not so "School Speech Day" on TV, she doesn't lean towards the interviewer as if she was handing out a prize. With confidence, she's developed this habit of "reflecting" with interviewers – staring at the carpet as if she's looking for something that's fallen on the floor. And now, just before she shoots from under the eyebrows, she's got this new habit of licking her lips, as if she was taking aim.

'The most fantastic thing about the woman is the way she answers a question straight through to the end. When she leaves blanks between her words, they're always silent blanks. I've never once heard Maggie "um" or "er". But have you noticed she's never been able to control her very bad habit of rushing at people, head first, at an angle of forty-five degrees, as if she was in a permanent hurry?'

I've not only noticed it, I once pointed out to Maggie that she sails towards her fellow world leaders, at summits, like the slanted figurehead on a man-o'-war, as if she's about to board them. She cut the ground from under my feet with 'If you had to get through my day, you'd go at it head first. If I look as if I'm in a hurry, it's because I am.'

After a decade as PM, the perfect English rose is still unwithered. If anything, her bloom seems fuller on an average five hours' snatched sleep a night. 'The Press boys would get a very different picture of me if they photographed me writing a speech at 4 a.m., running my hands through my upended hair.' Asked how she does it, when strong men in her Cabinet are dropping like flies, she'll tell you, 'The only secret is that I love this job. It suits me and stimulates me. Hard work is my life, my second nature. Even during the Falklands, when I couldn't snatch even the few hours of sleep I need because I was so desperately worried what could happen the next day, there's never been a moment when I've thought, "Oh, my goodness [she never, if ever, profanes God's name] I wish I wasn't here."'

It was during the Falklands she wept in her daughter Carol's arms, for the fallen, but wouldn't expect you to believe that. The only task in which she's painfully aware of failure is inspiring true, Churchillian love, even in those who vote for her. These days, the woman who told me fifteen years ago, 'Under all this, there's a bit of tough steel that's me,' realizes that the PM-ship which 'has grown on me, like a second skin', has hardened, in the country's eyes, into inbuilt armour.

Maggie is now seen as Old Iron, indestructible body and soul. She revels in her Iron Ladyship: 'Nobody patronizes me for being a woman – *nobody* puts me down' but, perversely, wants us to see the sincere, compassionate woman within who is very seldom allowed out.

A handful of times, on TV, she has shown her raw, astoundingly tender inner emotions. As a bowed, broken-hearted figure at the funeral of Airey Neave, her right-hand man killed by an IRA bomb. Laying a wreath at the burned-out Bradford football stand, her unkempt hair rain-lashed and her eyes red-rimmed. And speaking on a chat show – or rather unable to, for choking tears – about her loving debt to the late father she still worships.

In an emotional outburst to me, the only time one of our interviews has ground to a halt while she visibly pulled herself back together, she anguished, 'I'm absolutely amazed when people say I'm hard and uncaring, because it's so utterly untrue. I can't say it because, if you tell people you're caring, it's like saying "I'm a very modest person", nobody believes you. But it *does* hurt when I'm pilloried as cruel and unfeeling, because it's just not true,' said the woman who can face anything but her over-bearing, lounge-suited, cigar-smoking puppet on *Spitting Image*. 'I *do* care. And I don't know how to get it across. And I know that I *can't* get it across.'

Probably I can't either, but, if the pen is mightier than the politician's sword, I care enough for her to have a stab. To know the woman, as I do after hours of tape-recording her public and private feelings, is not slavishly to love her. Maggie can be very irritating. She's maddeningly bossy, down to headmistressy hints that you need a hair-cut, which you're obliged to take because she looks better-groomed, at the end of her eighteen-hour day, than you looked at the start of yours. She's amusingly nosey about your private life, which she can't resist reorganizing, annoyingly rather better than you had it yourself.

At her most self-confident, and that's most of the time, she can sound as stunningly arrogant as the Grantham schoolgirl who chopped off a teacher's comment, 'Lucky you, Margaret, to win the poetry prize' with a Miltonic, 'I was *not* lucky, I deserved it.' Or, as she once earnestly told me, 'I have to go on, it's as the twins say: "Mummy, there's no-one else with the same sort of purpose, drive and direction that you have." I know it sounds dreadful for me to say it, but they're right.' It sounded nearly as dreadfully epic as her comment when I asked if she would ever retire: 'Certainly not yet, my task is unfinished,' was the lordly reply which tempted me to remind her that she's not actually The Second Coming.

She is a true lioness, without a cowardly hair. The night of the Brighton bomb-blast which blew her hotel bathroom to smithereens, she appeared on the steps of the Imperial hotel, minutes later, fully dressed, and clad in iron courage among the torn nighties and crumpled dressing gowns. A living bronze Boadicea, in a scorched chariot of fire, she snorted defiance at the forces of evil: 'If I am to carry out my job, and I will carry it out, I will continue to live in danger.' So spoke, and acted, the great statesman. It was the brave woman who said, at a Thanksgiving service two days later, 'The sunlight was falling across the church on to some flowers, and it occurred to me that this is the day I was not meant to see.'

This woman can be loyal, warm-hearted, never forgetful of a favour, and a silent listener to others' troubles. When I interviewed her a month after I'd been brutally tied up and robbed by masked raiders, she shut the door of her attic flat, even on her own security guards, and urgently hugged me with, 'Now tell me all about it, and how you and the family are coping.'

Her waywardly snooty son – she should have sent him to snob-bashing Eton, not snob-making Harrow – is her Achilles' heel, and the only time she's sharply trodden on me is for column comments I've made on Mark. 'You'd hate to read it about your son, you'd feel just as I do, you'd be heart-broken.'

True. But I'd have broken Gresby's neck if, on the day of his engagement to the bimbettish blonde daughter of a Texan millionaire, he'd snapped at the press – who'd been courteously allowed to close in on the engagement rings of the Princess of Wales and the Duchess of York – 'You can't take a picture of her hand, this is a private matter.' Master Thatcher might consider that, to date, his only claim to fame is his mother's name which, unlike his hard-working twin, Carol, he doesn't hesitate to make public when he needs it to pull strings.

Unhappily, he doesn't take after his low-key father, or his mother who'll not only show you her not very flash thirty-seven-year-old engagement ring, but, when asked about the single pair of pearl earrings she's made world famous in thousands of photographs, unclips them and readily fills your palm with the lightweight ping-pong balls. 'They're not very good earrings, you know,' she said when she let me try them on to prove they don't pinch. 'Absolutely fake and quite cheap. I suppose one day the clips will go and I'll lose them.'

On the right hand which governs Britain, she always wears a bracelet of very semi-precious coloured stones, her first present from Denis, and 'my most valuable possession'. Maggie's sexual vibes are surprisingly, and to some men, overwhelmingly strong. Added to the ultimate aphrodisiac of her immense power, they easily have male members of her Cabinet falling at her feet, to be chastely flirted with. Maggie herself admits, 'I like to be made a fuss of by lots of chaps,' who are stomped into her Persian carpets if they get on the wrong side of her.

Her fellow world leaders are just as susceptible to the face Norman Mailer described as having 'the eyes of a Caligula above the mouth of a Marilyn Monroe'. France's President Mitterand was turned by Maggie into a bulging-eyed frog, hopping round her for favours; and, dancing within short range of her heat-seeking missile eyes, poor old Ronnie

Reagan seemed finally to have dropped all his marbles.

The only fearless man who can handle her, often has, and frequently still does, is Denis, who once saved the British press corps from being mown flat at a photo opportunity of Maggie driving a tractor by yelling, 'For Christ's sake look out, she's coming!'

The Thatchers were never Romeo and Juliet. Maggie was too blondely buxom for the part, and, even on his 1951 wedding day, Denis already looked like a balding golf ball. Mr and Mrs T. are apparently sensible stuff, of which romantic dreams are not made. You couldn't imagine a less Mills and Boon-like couple, or picture them in a double bed. The fact remains that Maggie adores the man who sent her into her PM-ship's most bloodily dangerous battle over the Westland affair, when she faced the House armed with her resignation, with, 'You'll be all right, love, you'll be all right.'

'I do not think I could have done it without Denis,' she said simply, on their thirty-fifth wedding anniversary. That day the world saw a whole new picture of Maggie, seated alongside Denis on a rose-coloured sofa. She never looked smaller or comfier, clinging to her man with her mouth wide open in one of her rare uproarious laughs, careless of showing her gums and the double chins we never knew she had. Her iron image melted, as she talked of her life's love affair with her now seventy-three-year-old partner. Admitting Denis occasionally sighs, 'Oh love, how much longer?' though he always says it in the same breath as, 'There really isn't anyone else, you know, so if you can keep going, so can I.'

She never looked less like a world leader, or what one US commentator once lyrically called 'a latter day goddess, with the pale blue light of diamonds in her eyes'. For an unguarded moment, she was housewifely, dependent, flustered. Mushy Maggie. The Passionate PM. Desire in Downing Street.

Then she made her most moving speech from the heart no-one could doubt. 'The whole feeling between us is for life. It's a great love story, a great friendship story, a great mutual interest story. It's everything – it's been thirty-five years. My love for Denis is a golden thread which runs through the days, through the weeks, through the months, and through the years.'

Listening to these touching words of undying love, I didn't know that the thread of my own marriage was already frayed, and soon about to snap.

CHAPTER ✦ THIRTEEN

The Cruellest Month

*I*nvolved as I was with my own survival, it was spring before I suddenly noticed a terrible change in Geoff. The craggy face of my husband of nearly twenty-five years had always looked well-worn and long-lived-in. When he rarely glanced in a mirror, Geoff used to joke, 'I wasn't born, I was hewn.' Even on our wedding day, my father remarked, without malice, 'He's got a fascinating face – like a cross between Puck and something chipped off Notre Dame.'

I'd grown so accustomed to the eternal rockery of Geoff's face, I never imagined it shifting. But April is the cruellest month. Its pale, probing sunshine peers into the cracks in everything and everybody. After my bleak winter, huddled in my own miseries, I looked closely at Geoff in the cold light of one April morning, and blinked at what I saw. Not only were there darker shadows, and deeper, hidden valleys in his face, but, more frighteningly, I began to sense great gloomy, empty spaces in his mind.

Geoff had always written things down. Memos to me, reminders to himself, jottings to Gresby. Our calendars were ringed with dates. Geoff's more important promptings to himself and everybody else were pinned among the postcards on a cork board in our kitchen. I used to complain there was more writing on our wall than at Belshazzar's Feast.

Now, what had been casual scrawling became an obsession. Increasingly slowly and laboriously, Geoff would write down shopping lists, work lists, notes to himself on where he was going which, when he'd been there, he meticulously ticked off. Writing lists, notes, memos and dates was no longer an aid to everyday living, but, in itself, a new and a terrible way of life. Since Geoff and I never had 'private' correspondence, I was free to read the piled-up sheets of spiral notebook scattered like a cloth on our kitchen table. Geoff began asking me, a dozen times a morning, 'What day is it?' Now I was alarmed to notice that all his scribblings – even a couple of supermarket items to be bought – were headed with the date, and the day of the week heavily underlined.

All the years I'd known him, Geoff had half-eaten *The Times* crossword with his breakfast, and always finished it over lunch. Now he would sit for hours, his face blank as the untouched squares. Attempts to rally him whipped up snappish aggression, or child-like apologies for 'being so forgetful these days'.

Never neat in his person – Geoff's clothes looked as if they'd been blown on by a passing wind – he was ex-Royal Navy shipshape about the house. A wonderfully handy man, who had DIY-ed me a fitted pine kitchen as a birthday present, Geoff's watchword on files, tidy drawers, and even old coffee jars full of neatly labelled nails, was 'a place for everything, and everything in its place'.

Overnight, everything in our sprawling, seven-bedroomed house was all over the place. Even the stairs were littered with battery-less torches and electric plugs which Geoff was systematically taking off our now useless appliances. In our loft, he had a half-finished model railway he'd tinker with on winter evenings. My roof fell in the afternoon I went up for a suitcase, and stepped into the debris of what looked like an appalling rail crash. Track was torn up, once precious little engines and coaches lay smashed on their sides in a tangle of wrenched and twisted wire. Standing among the wreckage, I had to accept that my husband, too, was rapidly falling apart.

Why the hell, you'll ask, as I've often asked myself, didn't I see the warning signs earlier that something was radically wrong inside Geoff's head? I suppose, shamefully, because I'd been so self-involved and, come to that, spent so much time in bed since Christmas. And, anyway, Geoff had regular check-ups for the acute bronchitis and emphysema with which he'd retired from the PA three years previously. He had been examined by his doctor, and his chest specialist, only six weeks before my terrible discovery in his railway room.

When the crash of Geoff's mind came, it was at lightning speed, and roaring all over us before we saw it coming. By the time he began to complain of 'terrible, buzzing headaches', they had diagnosed the 'massively aggressive' brain tumour which was to kill him.

During those painfully brief weeks before it did, Gresby and I had to wander with Geoff in the darkness which was closing all around him. Nothing we did or said suited him. The son whom he worshipped was held at arm's length, and then at the widening distance he was putting between himself and us.

Three days before I found the wrecked railway, Gresby rang from Eton – could Dad pick him up, usual time and place, after Sunday Chapel? When they came home, our son was as unusually quiet as our now wretched house, where Geoff insisted on sitting alone in his bedroom, staring, as we thought, at his TV.

In the late afternoon, Gresby began pottering around me. Could I drive him back to school that night instead of Dad? Yes, but why? Dad was free next day, I had to be early in Fleet Street, and, anyway, Dad was better at handling the suicidally overcrowded M25.

'Look, that's just it, he isn't any more,' said Gresby reluctantly. 'This morning he was weaving in and out of the lanes as if he was drunk. Twice we missed hitting another car by a whisker.'

'Gres, you're not scared of Dad's driving? He's the best, always has been,' I said, hit by yet another new and dreadful suspicion that we were all running out of road. 'I'm terrified,' said Gresby who, in the old days, would have driven with his father to the ends of the earth. 'It was bad enough in daylight. If he has to do it with lights, we'll all be killed.'

That settled the chauffeur, but how, without badly damaging him, was I to break it to Geoff that, for the first time in our son's boarding school life, he didn't want Dad to drive him back? Half an hour later Geoff came in from the garage and told me he had a puncture, so I'd have to drive to Eton.

In the light of the dark days to come, I believe that Geoff's vision was fading by the hour, and that he self-inflicted that puncture to protect Gresby's life. As I believe that for weeks, even months, before we or his doctors suspected it, Geoff guessed that his own life was coming to an end.

Later that day the garage picked up Geoff's punctured Range Rover, and then rang to ask what they should do about 'the other damage'. What other damage? 'About twelve hundred pounds' worth at a rough estimate,' the voice on the phone stunned me. 'Don't tell me you haven't noticed it?' It hit me that I hadn't seen the Range Rover on the forecourt for days. Untypically, Geoff had begun locking it in the garage out of sight.

The rail crash in the loft was nothing to what I found in the local garage workshop. Geoff's car looked like a wounded animal. Both rear lights and a headlamp were smashed, there was a Titanic rip, down to the already rusting metal, on the offside, and bumps, bangs and bashes on everything but the roof. Gresby must have known, but would never split on Dad. Now our embarrassed gardener admitted he hadn't wanted to upset me by letting on that, within one week, Geoff had hit the side of the house, lamp-posts, gates, fences, and carved up a stationary Volvo in the High Street, leaving a note to say he'd done it.

I tore back to the house and upstairs to Geoff's bedroom, not even knocking on the closed door through which his endless TV was blasting. And stopped, dry-mouthed, when I saw that Geoff was looking at nothing. All four channels were hopelessly untuned, and Geoff was gazing placidly at the dancing white spots on the screen.

I tried to calm my frenzy into some sort of focus by 'miraculously mending' the TV. 'But Geoff, you're doing it again!' I said, as he serenely began to wipe the screen by pressing every button on his remote control. I grabbed his twitching hands, and tried desperately to break through the thickening veil between me and my husband's once bright, alert mind.

'Geoff, the car, the railway room, you, everything, what the hell is going on in this benighted house?'

'Can you hear strange voices?' he said. There was nothing to hear but the once more scrambled TV.

We clung to each other's shaking hands. Suddenly, clearly, firmly, Geoff said, 'It's time I was out of it. I'm going the same way as my mother.' An hour later his diagnosis was confirmed by the doctor. Geoff had Alzheimer's disease, that slow, cruel crumbling of the mind. I believed it at the time, and so, briefly, did the doctor.

Looking back, I think that Geoff, who now knew so pitifully little of what was going on around him, knew better than anyone that his mental decay was not gradual, but something more monstrous, though mercifully quick. But we were all sidetracked by the memory of what had happened to Geoff's mother at the end of her life in the shockingly short space of three weeks. One weekend, when we dropped in at her pin-neat Rotherham home, where you could have eaten her first-rate cooking off her gleaming floors, she was as usual – Persil-white hair in a freshly made bun, scrubbed apple cheeks, and a spotless blouse straight from the ironing board. The next, we had a phone call from Rotherham's chief of police, an old chum of Geoff's. 'Can you come? We've just picked up Geoff's mother from a traffic island in the middle of the A1. She and the dog were having a picnic. She said, "It's such a nice place to watch the cars go by."'

We dashed north to find the door locked, curtains closed, and a Greek tragedy of a scene behind them. While we hammered, and the dog inside howled, Geoff's mother appeared, like one of the Trojan Women, wild-eyed, with her white hair streaming to her shoulders. Every light bulb in the house had been removed. As we sat in the gathering gloom of her deranged mind, she told us 'Edward took them out for safety'. Edward was Geoff's father, dead for twenty years. 'I wish you could have met him, but he's gone fishing,' she smiled at me. 'Who are you?' She died shortly after in a nursing home, knowing neither of us.

Now her son seemed to be vanishing down the same dark, meandering road. Premature senility like his mother's had been Geoff's greatest terror, and I knew he was inwardly howling, like Lear, above the storm of his brain, 'O! let me not be mad, not mad, sweet heaven.'

All he said, when the doctor left, was, 'I'm useless, kid. It's time I was under the sod.' I had to smile at this gnarled old Yorkshire-ism. Geoff had never come completely South. After twenty-five years, he still asked for a 'spice' instead of a sweet, and cracked me up, during explicit TV sex operas, with, 'Hey, sithee! – a lass wi' nowt on!'

'You're not going under any sod,' I said. 'Don't you remember we're moving with the times and having each other cremated? You're supposed to chuck my ashes off the Humber Bridge.'

'You can fling mine out of the car window in Rotherham instead,' he said. It was one of his last flashes of humour, or of sense.

Strictly forbidden by the chest specialist to smoke, I knew that secretly he did. Now that he could no longer sneak down the garden, I found alarming scorch marks on carpets and sheets. Unless closely watched, Geoff would cremate us both, for free.

That night, thanking God Gresby was away at school, I slept on the bedroom floor. Geoff, who'd taken to wandering everywhere at all hours, would have to trip over me before he fell downstairs and broke his neck. Though, lying in the dark, monitoring my husband's breathing in his deeper, more dreadful darkness, I knew he would have begged me, in his right mind, to push him over the edge.

Next morning, all hell and Geoff's limbs broke loose. Within two terrifying hours, he lost all sense of balance or where-abouts. This, dammit, I rang the doctor and the psychiatrist who'd now examined him, was not senile decay. This was a hideous takeover by some inner, gigantic, and evil force. In God's name what was it? Though I already guessed.

Could I get Geoff to Maidstone Hospital – not to put too fine a point on it, what used to be called the local lunatic asylum? Only for psychological evaluation, they promised, swearing to me that he'd be almost immediately moved to a neurological hospital.

Driving Geoff from his home for the last time, I watched his face in the mirror. As the spring leaves danced shadows across it, it was puzzled, but calm. A child on the final mystery tour.

Within hours they moved him from Maidstone to Brook Hospital at Woolwich, a leading neurological centre. A biopsy of his brain showed a ballooning tumour. Had we found it earlier, I agonized, could anything have been done? Nothing. The tumour was 'massively aggressive and malignant', and the brain is a solid box. Unlike the breast, you can't cut unwanted lumps off it.

Could they do anything now? Nothing, but did I want radiotherapy? Was there the slightest, faintest, wildest hope that radiotherapy could save him? None. Then what was the point of it? A few extra weeks, and the satisfaction of knowing I'd done all I could.

Scrap that wretched and selfish satisfaction. I had gone through the hell of radiotherapy to be cured. Geoff was not going to be put through it just for the exercise. The consultant looked relieved by my snap decision. 'How long?' I asked him.

'Six months at the outside, more likely two.' When I saw

Geoff after the biopsy, his head completely shaved, and with no more mind than hair, I prayed for two minutes.

Twisted and terrible days followed when Geoff was convinced he was being followed by the IRA, even the Russians. For twenty-four appalling hours he was desperately agitated at the notion of being set down in Gatwick Airport, at the wrong time and gate, for the wrong plane.

Watching him staring at me as if I held some secret of release from this torture, I thought we would both run madder than Lear. One day, desperate for something to say, I asked, 'Geoff, is there anything I can do, buy, fetch, anything you want, anything at all I can get you?' The sudden, brief, but absolutely lucid light in his blue eyes was quite beautiful. 'Jean,' he smiled, 'what a bloody stupid thing to say!'

They mercifully suggested he come home to our local cottage hospital to die. Two rooms from the room in which he had visited me in hospital six months before, Geoff sat among the June roses waiting, not patiently, for the end. Note-making to the last, in one of his old reporter's notebooks, he wrote the day before he died, on the right-hand side of the page which was all he could see, 'Life today has been frightening – thank goodness it is nearly over.'

To shrink the tumour, and keep up his strength, he was on steroids. They considered stopping them. Please, please. I realized he would 'sink very quickly'. Please, please! He sank like a stone. Within hours, the fretful misery of his life was passing peacefully into a coma. The veil between us was hardening into the iron curtain of death. Just before it fell, I held him close and told him what he most needed to hear.

I told him he was not, never had been mad. His killer had been physical, not mental. I would be fine – fit as a flea, you know me, I'd live to be a Dame if I hadn't written all that stuff about the Royals. And of course Gresby would pass maths O-level for the third time of asking, and be the first Lord Chancellor to play for Rotherham United.

His wordless smile, and his string-thin arm round my neck,

were enough. That was Friday morning. Saturday, at 11 p.m., he was still incredibly alive. The next day was to have been our silver wedding anniversary. I had to get home, lock up, and take the dog, but dare I leave? 'My dear, you could sit here all night, or he could go the moment your hand's on the car door handle,' said the sweet Sister. 'Do you need to see him die?'

No, but I needed to be with him at midnight, as our twenty-five years of marriage rolled by to its close. If Geoff was going to wait for our silver wedding, I would be there. I flew back from a brief stop at the house. At 1.30 a.m. I said what I knew would be my last goodbye, certain that Geoff would not want me to watch him leave. He died at ten minutes to 4 a.m.

I had no doubts who were my husband's primary killers. They were the three masked men who burst into our house one wild winter night in 1985, knocked us around for an hour, snatched our silver and my jewellery, and robbed Geoff of his confidence and strength, which he never regained after that night.

On the afternoon of the break-in I'd dragged myself back from Los Angeles, with a 'flu bug which had felled half of Hollywood. Geoff and I had had separate bedrooms since the first year of our marriage. For six months we'd shared my unsociable working hours, plus Geoff's Press Association shifts – 7 a.m. to 3 p.m., 5 p.m. to midnight, 11 p.m. to dawn – until we were worn out as our restless double bed. If our marriage cracked up because we didn't sleep together except at whoopee weekends, tough. We would crack up unless we got some sleep.

At 8 p.m. I crashed into my four poster, so jet-and-'flu-lagged I could hardly speak or see. At 9.30 Geoff dropped by to say he was taking the dog out. Should he call in before he went to bed? 'God, no,' I wheezed. 'Just let me die – and don't get so near me, whatever I've got, you and the dog don't want.'

Around 10 o'clock I was dredged from a doze by a torch

shining in my face. Seconds later, it wavered from the room and the door softly closed.

Our rambling Victorian house, isolated on a Kent hilltop, has a thirty-foot landing. Doped and exasperated, I flung wide my bedroom door and bawled at the tall, thin figure at the far end of the landing, 'Geoff, if you're going to keep checking I'm still alive, don't shine your torch on me!' The thin shape flitted down the landing, at top speed, towards the door I was already closing. I hadn't seen Geoff move so fast in years. Except that it wasn't Geoff. . . .

The torch, again full on my face, began to revolve like a mad, miniature moon, blinding me. 'Geoff, what the hell are you doing? Geoff, are you drunk or what, stop it!' The lowered torch stopped, and I looked straight into the eyeless holes of a woollen balaclava. 'Do as I say, or I'll kick your fucking head in!' said the faceless man bending over my bed. 'Get up, and shut up!'

My shaking hand was within six inches of the panic switch in the wall which would have set our alarm screaming from the hilltop. I had a second to decide whether to hit it, and have had years to wonder if I could have saved our possessions, had I dared.

I'd probably have lost our lives. Two thoughts tied my hands. If I did turn the alarm key I couldn't get rid of it, I'd have to swallow it. And where was Geoff? Because, if he was able to reach me, he wouldn't have let this man get to me. Somebody else in the house must be holding Geoff, and my throwing the alarm might scare whoever it was into finishing him off.

Another masked man burst into the room, reeking of sweat, the mud on his wet feet, and his own terror. Strange how the smell of fear is as strong on the robber as on his victim. Stockier, and mentally thicker than the first raider, whom he addressed as 'Number One', Number Two was having sick fun with me. Holding me by the hair, he flicked my face with a leather glove, the eyeholes of his woollen mask boring down the front of my nightgown.

'This is it!' snapped Number One, ripping open the drawers

in which my fantastically vast collection of gold jewellery – often, too often, seen on TV – gleamed from its partitions. It had taken me thirty years to gather it from every part of the world. Within minutes, my little golden world had gone – China, Japan, India, all Europe, America, Africa, Australia, tumbling and jangling into a pillowcase.

Frustrated and frantically clawing at the back of the drawers, the stocky man yelled, 'I'll smash your fucking face in unless you give me the diamonds!' What diamonds? He wasn't robbing Elizabeth Taylor. Like millions of middle-aged women, the only diamond I had was the smallish five-stone ring put on my finger twenty-two years previously.

'There goes my wedding day,' I thought, idiotically less annoyed that they now had me down on my hands and knees, tightening a wire round my neck, than that they'd nicked my clean-on flowered pillowcases. But what in hell had they done to my husband?

When they dragged me backwards down the stairs by my hair, Geoff, lashed with wire to a bench in the back hall, snarled at them, and tried to spring. 'Why on earth didn't you put the alarm on?' I snapped at him, treasuring him more at that moment than the life I thought we would lose, but ever the familiar, nagging wife.

'It wouldn't have done any good, they jumped me outside with the dog,' he said, wanting to murder them for touching me, but ever the righteous husband with a logical excuse for making a mess of it. At least, I thought wryly, normal married life goes on – while it lasts.

'If you value that dog, you'll shut up, both of you,' said one of the horrifying, hooded faces. Are they normal, these people? After they'd finished with us, would they go for a beer? Our distraught, seven-months-old cocker spaniel, Jo, was Gresby's Christmas present. We valued her as much as anything in the pillowcases, so we shut up, and put up.

I'll say this for our robbers, they weren't vandals. They smashed nothing but our psyches. 'Number One' even covered my now 100-plus temperature with a coat, put my slippers on, called me a 'good, brave girl', kissed me on the cheek, and actually apologized for 'what you must think is a terrible thing, but it's a terrible world, isn't it? Anyway, you have everything, and we've got nothing.'

We had nothing now for which we, and our parents before us, had worked like dogs – except our shattered lives which at least would be more valuable to Gresby than the family heirlooms. 'What about a car?' they asked Geoff. 'Take my Rover in the middle garage,' I said, robbed blind but still commercially minded. Geoff's car was his own, the *Express* would replace mine.

With a final flash of the torch, they were gone. So had everything. Geoff and I were lashed together by our wired wrists, back to back on the hall floor, in a howling gale from the open door which would take about five minutes to whip my 'flu into pneumonia. 'Don't move,' he grunted, as my car dwindled down the drive.

'I wasn't going to,' I said. 'I feel as if I'm welded to you, and the bloody dog's sitting on my face.'

'I think I can get us out of it if I break my wrist,' said Geoff, as if tackling DIY. 'Trouble is, I might break yours.'

'I'm dying of cold anyway, so go ahead,' I said. Excruciating minutes later, Geoff was free, if sprained and bleeding, and on the phone to the police.

The police were more exhausting than our robbers. They spent five hours grilling us on details of our lost property, and six months getting nowhere, and getting nothing back. They actually arrested three suspects, one of whose girlfriends had grassed, but since their hands were comparatively clean, had to let them go. Not long after, we read a description in the local paper of a three-man raid, identical in method to our own, on another Kent country house.

By now it was 4 a.m., and TV-am, lights blazing on our front door, was shrieking through the keyhole for an interview. The phone was so blocked, we took it off the hook, ringing Gresby at Eton at 7 a.m., only to find he'd just heard it on LBC News, and was all for coming home with a shotgun.

In the next three months I came nearer to breaking down

than I thought possible, and remember one day crouching on the floor, screaming at the *Express*, 'I can't come in to work, and I won't!' while a gentle voice at the other end tried to soothe me, 'Jean, we're not even asking you to.'

One afternoon, I sat on the bed, shaking more with rage now than terror, and thought, 'The bastards had everything else – they're not having my job.' I pulled myself together, wrote my anguish out of my system, and spilled it to Anne Diamond on TV-am. Everyone showered me with sympathy, champagne and flowers, all our friends thought of me. Nobody realized the toll it had taken on Geoff.

For ten days after the robbery, Geoff and I sat, for no logical reason, on the back stairs down which they'd dragged me, drinking too much of the *Express*'s compassionate champagne, and talking and smoking our heads off. Geoff had at that time been genuinely smokeless for two years. Now he was back on sixty lethal cigarettes a day, but I hadn't the heart to nag him.

Life for Geoff was never the same. After the night of the robbery it seemed to drain out of him. Only I heard his almost nightly, yelling nightmares, reliving the moment he'd been jumped on from behind. I never knew, because he wouldn't talk about it, how hard they hit him on the head that night, or even if they hit him at all. They didn't need to. Once and forever, those godless swine had knocked the stuffing out of him.

Within weeks, the sharp, street-wise reporter, and 140 w.p.m. shorthand writer, was talking about early retirement. 'Geoff, you'll loathe it, you know you will. You'll die without The Street after all these years. I agree your chest's not up to door-stopping in the rain any more, but they've offered you a good desk job. Why not take it?'

He was stubbornly hell-bent on retiring, not only from his work, but from active life. The night he left Fleet Street, after twenty-two years as a crack PA reporter, the pubs were choked. His colleagues gave him a silver tankard, inscribed 'MFL' – the PA reporter's abbreviation to his news desk for 'more follows later. . . .'

Nothing followed later. Geoff never once looked back, or went back to Fleet Street, on which he'd lived for so long, or looked up any of his once close colleagues. Though dozens of them who loved him wrote glowingly after his death, and two PA editors came to his funeral. He seemed to have taken his last train from London to nowhere. His desultory days were spent reading newspapers, or gossiping in the local pubs. All work in and around the house stopped. After the October 1987 hurricane, in which millions of Kent's trees went with the 110 m.p.h. wind, Geoff could have cleaned up with colour stories on the aftermath. He never wrote a line. It was as if he had died three years previously, and his shell had dragged on through the aimless time left.

At 7 a.m. the day Geoff died, I rang our son. 'Dad?'

'Dad's gone. It's best for him, Gres. Wish him God speed, but don't wish him back.' I collected Geoff's bits and pieces from the hospital. The watch he'd taken off every day that final week to 'give to Gresby', and which I'd strapped back round his bone-thin wrist. His spectacles, wrapped in a spiral notebook marked for me.

'I can't bear to read this,' I begged the hospital to burn Geoff's last words, now that I could no longer reply. 'We had to read it before we gave it to you – it's wonderful, you'll want to keep it,' they assured me.

I took the notebook home and set it at Geoff's empty place at the kitchen table. 'Not now,' I pleaded. 'Not now, when I can't answer you.' I read all his notes, in longhand and still copperplate shorthand, right down to, 'Don't forget we've some blue paint left over in the boiler room.' And his last love letter, written a month before his death, which began, 'It has been made pretty clear to me today that my life is a matter of months, if that. . . .'

I turned my car round and drove slowly, calmly back to the hospital. I had to see Geoff again, and I wasn't going to be put off by the urging of the undertaker, who'd called mid-morning, 'I really think you should wait until we've had him for a little while. You shouldn't go straight down and see him there.' But I didn't want to see craggy Geoff, tarted up and lying on satin. I knew the hospital 'chapel' was just a cheap wooden cross above a plank in a hut, but it would do.

In thirty years in journalism, I'd somehow avoided viewing a dead body, and my beloved father had warned that he'd haunt me if I attempted to view him – 'Remember me as I was'. When the nurse unlocked the door on the sheeted figure, I was braced to bolt.

I thought of Geoff's hilarious descriptions of his cub reporting days in Rotherham, when he was always invited to see the departed, and actually pressed by one woman to 'Rest your notebook on the coffin, love, he won't mind.' 'They always said the same thing: "Doesn't 'e look peaceful?"' grinned Geoff. 'Did he hell look peaceful. He looked like a corpse.'

'Doesn't he look peaceful?' whispered the nurse. Twenty-five years to the day since I had married him, I bent to kiss Geoff's cold cheek. I was glad I'd seen him. 'But did you hell look peaceful, Geoff,' I was forced to smile in the car. 'You looked like a corpse.'

All that had been Geoff was long gone. What was left of him we despatched as simply as he would have wished. We sang the old Yorkshire hymn, 'Lead, Kindly Light, amid the encircling gloom,' which said it all about the dreadful four months it took him to die. The curtains finally closed on him to a rousing chorus of 'Ilkley Moor, baht 'at'.

The Tuesday after Geoff died, my column day, nobody expected a word from me. At 6 a.m. our chilly, undusted, paper-littered kitchen looked like the *Sheffield Telegraph* in the early hours of the morning. I poured a coffee, lit a cigarette, and wrote:

Regular readers of this column have been in, for seventeen years, on my family joys and sorrows. From the birth of our son to the death of our Great Dane, and through the nightmare when we were robbed by masked raiders.

So it will help me to tell you that my husband, Geoffrey Nash, died last Sunday, on our silver wedding anniversary. Over thirty years ago, when I was an eager, hugely plump cub reporter and Geoff was my deputy news editor on the *Sheffield Telegraph*, he asked me what I wanted out of journalism.

'To have my picture, and my name in mile-high type on top of a column in the *Daily Express*,' I told him, as we sat in our dingy local Yorkshire office, regarding my brilliant future in the muddy dregs of our paper coffee cups. 'You can do it,' my future husband convinced me. 'I couldn't do it myself, but I can show you how.'

Our marriage was not the century's flawless love story. Like millions, we had our thrilling front-page ups, and our mean and petty downs you wouldn't want to read about. But, up to last week's Wimbledon, as from my first wild young dreams in Sheffield, Geoff was always behind my typewriter.

Never minding that he himself was nothing but what he wanted to be – an unsung, lowly paid, totally professional agency reporter who seldom saw his name even in small type.

Among all the years of his flat, unfailing Yorkshire advice, I most treasure his comment on my hysterical eve of Prince Charles's marriage. 'Remember it's only another wedding write-up. Once you've said what the bride wore, noticed if the groom's mother cried, listed the bridesmaids, and let rip on the distinguished guests, you're half way there,' he said. 'You can do it.'

Next week I'm taking our son on a long holiday. But today it seemed important to me to prove to myself – by myself – that I can still do it. I hope my pen has been unwavering and sharp. Even if not, I am proud that this column has been written, with extra effort, by JEAN NASH.

For the umpteenth time in my life, I rang my paper, and dictated my copy. Then I marked the original 'For the attention of Geoff Nash, deputy news editor from Rook, staff', and took it to the funeral home to be placed in Geoff's coffin.

The morning after the funeral, I flew off with Gresby and

one of his schoolfriends to Italy. On our return, I drove to Yorkshire to scatter Geoff's ashes, without much hope, since I've no sense of direction, of finding Ulley, the speck of a village where we had done our 'courting'. His son, handy as Dad with an Ordnance Survey map, found even the narrow, grass-grown country lane where Geoff and I used to make love in his beat-up old Morris.

'Do you want to be with me?' I asked Gresby.

'No.'

It was between me and Dad. I flung Geoff's ashes into the hedgerows which had overlooked our passionate outpourings. As his silver dust settled, I looked back up the road at his son, standing terribly alone.

In the last seven months Gresby had gone through hell – his mother's cancer, his father's personality change, and death. Worst for him now, but best in the long run, he hadn't gone to see his father at the end. Wisely, he hadn't wanted to, he wanted to forget the past mad weeks, and remember his father as the craggy old rock who had hung, besotted, over his pram, and their man-to-man holidays together in Cornwall and Ireland. I prayed daily he wouldn't ask to go to the hospital. I couldn't bear him to watch his father shrinking into a demented elf.

All three of us had suffered desperately in those months before we knew the truth – the misunderstanding, bickering, withdrawals, and utter confusion. Eton had compassionately offered Gresby the chance to duck Trials, their vital end of term exams. He told me, halfway down the M25, 'I'm going to take them, but if Dad dies just before, I'll fail.'

'Dad won't die,' I promised. I was convinced that Geoff, who knew about the exam, would hold on for his son's sake. Gresby took Trials, and his elusive maths O-level, and passed.

'All right, Gres?' I asked, as he mapped us out of Rotherham and back to the M1.

'All right,' he said with that calm dignity which neither over-sensitive Geoff, nor my over-ambitious, pushy self had ever achieved.

Gresby, I thought, is the best of both of us. Our son is the future, and the celebration of all that was happiest and finest in our past. And it *is* all right. . . .

WHAT I TRUST IS NOT
... THE EPILOGUE

I was kneeling again in Eton College chapel, among the hopeful young voices, and the timeless stone. Surely the echoes of last Christmas's carol concert, such a short time ago, must still be ringing in the vaulted roof? Two nights later, I had found cancer. Seven months later, I lost Geoff.

But I wasn't kneeling now, finding God to wipe away my tears. Or playing hell with Him for what He had done to me. I'm not a religiously subtle soul. My prayers are simple stuff – time to spend with Gresby, and strength to work.

If Gres achieves his aim to be a latter-day Laurence Olivier with a heavy metal guitar, he can keep me. I hope to see my grandchildren and, at the rate of my son's direct and rapid approach to girls, I won't need to linger all that long.

When you walk with cancer for a year, you stop glancing round to check if 'the fearful fiend doth close behind your tread', ready to lay its bony hand on your shoulder. You cross to the sunnier side of the street.

Learn to live in the shadow and love the sun more.

Sometimes my shadows are so short, I forget they're still on my heels. At some darker moments, they are long and strong, leaping at me from every corner of the bedroom, measuring the time I have left.

Some critic of this book will refer to 'her battle against cancer'. There's been no battle. Braver folk than I may 'take on' and 'fight' cancer, I wouldn't dare to tempt the Unseen Enemy. I accept that it and I will play Russian Roulette for the rest of my life but just hope its pistol remains jammed. It's presumptuous to triumph over cancer. While your luck holds and you're winning, best to shut up and just enjoy it.

Has it changed me? Not for the saintlier, or even the more sensible – I still smoke, drink, professionally push myself past the limits, and work killing hours. But everyday pleasures mean much more, and are more sharply etched on me. Gresby's profile. Frosted moonlight. The gloriously cheap thrill of ironing, scented hot baths, and pushing a piled-up supermarket trolley.

I enjoy the sun more. The Greek sun, which I thought never to see again, burning hotter than radiotherapy on my grateful back. A Kent sunset on a recent drive back from the cancer hospital. I was once a blindly, blazingly ambitious woman who would not park her high-powered Jag on the side of a road near Tunbridge Wells, just to watch a flaming sunset . . . I do now.

A friend of mine who read the first chapter of this book while I was writing the last, seven months later, laid it down shivering, 'Aren't you frightened?' I wasn't the moment before she said that but, yes, now she came to mention it, I'm scared rigid.

But not all the precious time. Mostly, I recognize despair, but live in hope. So if you are fearful of life, or dealing with death, take my outstretched paw. You cannot be more cowardly than this lioness. Mouse-scared at times. But ever optimistic, and roaring on.

Index